The Romance of New England Antiques

The Romance of New England Antiques

EDWIN VALENTINE MITCHELL

Current Books, Inc.
A. A. WYN, PUBLISHER
New York, 1950

Copyright 1950 by Edwin Valentine Mitchell

All rights reserved

Printed in the United States of America
American Book–Knickerbocker Press, Inc., New York

For
Elinor and Bill Wilde

Contents

1. The Romance of Collecting — 13
2. Old Curiosity Shops and Antique Dealers — 29
3. Going Going Gone: Town and Country Auctions — 41
4. Reproductions, Fakes, and Thefts — 53
5. Secret Hiding Places — 71
6. Antiques with a Pinch of Salt: The Seaport Towns and What to Look for There — 89
7. Yankee Whittlers — 105
8. Tinware and Yankee Peddlers — 117
9. Timepieces — 135
10. Concerning Chests — 157
11. Chairs — 171
12. A Silvery Metal Called Pewter — 187
13. Silverware — 203
14. Old New England Glasshouses — 221
15. New England Pottery — 239
16. The Story behind Them — 253

Acknowledgments

Grateful acknowledgment is made to Michael Wenick, antique dealer and auctioneer of Hartford, Connecticut, for much valuable information included in this book.

I am also deeply indebted to the late James M. Strong, whose knowledge of and interest in antiques was deep and abiding.

I am under particularly heavy obligation to Barrows Mussey, who not only loaned me numerous books, but also supplied me with notes about his experiences as a collector of antiques.

For special information I wish to thank Miss Elva B. McCormick, Mrs. P. M. Stone, Norman Snow, Paul Dole, Henry T. Kneeland, Robert C. Beers, and Jean Mitchell Boyd.

My thanks are also due to Terry West Mitchell.

E. V. M.

The Romance of New England Antiques

I

The Romance of Collecting

COLLECTING antiques, as we understand it today, is a relatively new thing. It began at the time of the celebration of the one hundredth anniversary of American independence in 1876. On May 11th of that year the Centennial Exhibition was opened at Fairmount Park in Philadelphia by President Grant. The Emperor of Brazil was present and the exercises included the playing of the "Centennial March," composed by Richard Wagner, the singing of the "Centennial Hymn," written by John Greenleaf Whittier, and a cantata by Sidney Lanier. By the time the Exhibition closed in November, upwards of nine million people, or some six million more than were in the original thirteen colonies at the time of the Revolution, had visited it. It was an international affair, but the displays of American historical relics and the industrial exhibits showing our material progress stimulated national pride and awakened interest in the past.

There were local observances of the anniversary everywhere, and many towns which had never had their history written were inspired to have it done. This was fortunate from the point of view of the present-day collector, as it is to these parochial volumes that one must occasionally resort to find out about the makers of antiques. If, for example, you should acquire a grandfather clock by a maker who is merely listed in a catalogue of craftsmen, you may, by consulting the history of the town where he worked, sometimes learn particulars concerning him which add to the interest of owning one of his timepieces.

Recently a relative of mine became the owner of a tall clock with the name of Frederic Wingate of Augusta, Maine, etched on the dial. A fine example, it seemed worth while to try to find out something about the maker and an old history of Augusta yielded an interesting story. Briefly, Frederic Wingate migrated from Haverhill, Massachusetts, to Augusta in 1804. He was then twenty-three years old, a full-fledged maker of brass-movement clocks just out of his apprenticeship. Clocks were not common in Maine then, and the arrival of one in a neighborhood was something of an event. People from all around came to see it.

A clockmaker named Nathaniel Hamlen had been making tall-case clocks with wooden movements in Augusta, some of which he sold without cases as wags-on-the-wall, but brass clocks were rarely seen. General Henry Sewall bought one in Boston, which he hired Hamlen to set up. The room in which it was placed was so low that a hole had to be cut in the ceiling to receive

The Romance of Collecting

the top ornaments. Afterward, says the Augusta historian, as clocks multiplied, it was not unusual when houses were built to provide a recess in the ceiling to accommodate their towering heads.

During his long career Wingate made many clocks for the settlers up and down the Kennebec River. His first sale was to Ezekiel Page. Page wanted a clock, but hesitated to order one, as he did not know how to take care of it. Wingate told Mr. Page that if he would buy a clock from him, he would call once a week to wind it and teach the family how to take care of it. Accordingly, the order was given and in due time the clock was installed in the Page home and Wingate commenced his weekly visits. These became more frequent when the young clockmaker began instructing Mr. Page's daughter Hannah in the mystery of caring for the clock. The clock kept perfect time, but the youth said that as it was his first one he liked to drop in often to see that it was running properly. Hannah began to look forward to his visits. She loved the clock and presently found that she loved its maker too. And on January 12, 1806, the clockmaker and his pupil were married and lived together happily for nearly sixty years. She died on March 8, 1864, aged seventy-nine, and he survived her only a few months. He was eighty-three when he died, on November 16th of that same year. His first clock brought Frederic Wingate his wife, and in reviewing his long life and the many transactions and bargains he had entered into, he was fond of saying that the first one was the best he ever made.

In looking through old town histories one's curiosity

is often aroused by coming across a paragraph like the following from the history of the town of Sutton, Massachusetts, a book written and published as a direct result of the Centennial.

> Pliny Slocumb was one of the assessors in this town. He was a Freemason, belonged to the Sutton Lyceum, and was skilled in debate. He was an artist, an ornamental painter, and one of the fastest workmen to be found. His sleighs, chairs, cradles, settees, etc., were much sought after for their fanciful ornamentation. One of his sons, too, was an artist, and painted a panorama, with which he traveled. Mr. Slocumb gave some attention to fruit growing, and made choice wines, on which he realized a handsome profit.

Entries of that kind about an artist or craftsman often serve as clues to the workmanship of pieces found in a particular locality.

The first antique collectors in the modern sense were New Englanders. One of the great pioneers was Dr. Irving W. Lyon of Hartford, Connecticut, whose book, *The Colonial Furniture of New England*, published in 1891, is still one of the best books on the subject. He began in 1877 to collect furniture in and around Hartford, a region rich at that time in the carved oaken woodwork of the seventeenth century. There were then a few others quietly engaged in the same pursuit and the number of collectors gradually increased in other parts of New England.

There had been some public interest in the things of the past long before this, but it was confined chiefly to historical relics, and not much attention was given to old

The Romance of Collecting

survivals as examples of American craftsmanship or expressions of folk art. There were museums with collections in the early years of the nineteenth century, mostly in seaport towns, the exhibits consisting principally of foreign curiosities fetched from far places by Yankee seafarers. Innkeepers and shopkeepers sometimes had collections to attract trade. James Russell Lowell has left a pleasant picture of the barbershop in Cambridge, Massachusetts, which he used to patronize in the days of his youth when that city was a village. It was like an old curiosity shop, and the boy who was to be shorn was invariably accompanied to the sacrifice by his friends, who were thus enabled to view the collection free.

> The sunny little room, fronting south-west upon the Common, rang with canaries and Java sparrows, nor were the familiar notes of robin, thrush, and bobolink wanting. A large white cockatoo harangued vaguely, at intervals, in what we believed to be the Hottentot language. . . . The walls were covered with curious old Dutch prints, beaks of albatross and penguins, and whales' teeth fantastically engraved. There was Frederick the Great, with head drooping plottingly, and keen side-long glance from under the three-cornered hat. There hung Buonaparte, too, the long-haired, haggard general of Italy, his eyes sombre with prefigured destiny; and there was his island grave;—the dream and the fulfillment. Good store of sea-fights there was also; above all, Paul Jones in the *Bonhomme Richard:* the smoke rolling courteously to leeward, that we might see him dealing thunderous wreck to the two hostile vessels, each twice as large as his own, and the reality of the scene corroborated by

streaks of red paint leaping from the mouth of every gun. Suspended over the fireplace, with the curling-tongs, were an Indian bow and arrows, and in the corners of the room stood New Zealand paddles and war-clubs, quaintly carved. The model of a ship in glass we variously estimated to be worth from a hundred to a thousand dollars. . . . Among these wonders, the only suspicious one was an Indian tomahawk, which had too much the peaceful look of a shingling-hatchet. Did any rarity enter the town, it gravitated naturally to these walls, to the very nail that waited to receive it, and where, the day after its accession, it seemed to have hung a lifetime.

Significant of the interest in antiques which began to flower shortly after the Centennial was the publication in 1881 of a long poem by Mary D. Brine called "Grandma's Attic Treasures." With its numerous wood engravings, it became a popular gift book which sold well for years. It tells of the new fad for antiques and how a couple of slick city dealers call at the old homestead and pay Grandma fifty dollars for the "rubbidge" in her attic and for furniture in other parts of the house. She is pleased to make the sale, because it enables her to buy a new bonnet and shawl and her husband to buy a new "cow-critter." She thinks the men are lunatics to buy her outmoded things, but presently she begins to miss some of her old possessions, particularly a small table, which the illustrations show to have been a gate-leg. She goes to visit her granddaughter in the city, who has an elegant town house stuffed with Victorian atrocities. Amid the flowered carpets, the sculptured figures

The Romance of Collecting

on marble pedestals, the potted plants in jardinieres, the ornate furniture, and the terrific chandeliers, Grandma spots a simple old table that looks out of place in such opulent surroundings. Examining it more closely, she discovers that it is her own dear old table. Her granddaughter explains that the new fashion is for old-fashioned things, for antiques that are as old as the hills, and tells her further that she paid more than fifty dollars for the table. This, of course, makes Grandma very, very angry at the "cheatin', deceivin' creeturs" who bought her things, but she is glad to find her table again, and goes home rejoicing. It is a sentimental poem full of fake homespun features, but coming when it did it may have put some old ladies on their guard against the wiles of dealers and collectors.

Actually, however, there were not many collectors or dealers during the horse-and-buggy age. There was a definite interest in antiques, and they were plentiful and cheap, but the demand for them was limited. This continued for almost two decades of the present century. Then in 1918, following World War I, there was a sudden upsurgence of interest. In the twinkling twenties new shops sprang up everywhere, in town and country. Business boomed and prices soared. The magazine *Antiques*, the first publication of its kind, made its appearance in Boston. In 1924 the American Wing of the Metropolitan Museum was opened with its period rooms, including a number of New England interiors. In 1928 the first antique show was held in New York.

Collecting antiques conferred distinction on the collector. The ownership of old things became a test of social acceptance. An antique might be useful or interesting on account of its historical associations, but it was also admired for its beauty, and that beauty was measured largely by its cost. One heard on all sides such remarks as "It's a beautiful example, isn't it? I gave three hundred and fifty for it," or "It's worth a thousand, but I only paid five hundred." To the true collector a thing is beautiful or not regardless of its price. It was a situation which must have interested Thorstein Veblen, as it was a perfect example of his economic theory of conspicuous waste. He died in 1929 just as the financial world came tumbling about our ears, wiping out a myriad of collectors.

Since World War II there has been another upswing, and the interest in antiques is now greater than ever before, but it is a more intelligent interest. The average collector of today is far better informed than the amateur connoisseur of the Harding and Coolidge era. The attendance figures at museums, galleries, and sale rooms are evidence of the keen interest taken by collectors. It is only necessary to look over the books about antiques which have been published during the last twenty-five years to see how much knowledge has been gained. Almost every branch of collecting has its own special literature. Collectors with the same interests meet to exchange information. It is no longer enough that an object is merely old. The present-day collector wants to know when, where, how, and by whom it was made. Its historical associations fascinate him. His imagination is stirred and he realizes that it is what he sees behind an object that counts as much as anything.

The Romance of Collecting

Dislike of the present is one of the reasons given for this interest in things of the past. Collecting antiques is alleged to be a form of escapism. Every antique, of course, is escapist in the sense that it summons you away from this world to one of its own. But people are by nature collectors. Most of us find it impossible not to acquire more than we need of certain things. There is hardly a man who has not a secret accumulation of ties or other articles. The urge to collect is so strong as to amount practically to a human instinct. Almost everyone begins in early youth, perhaps with marbles or postage stamps or birds' nests, passing from these to other forms of collecting as his tastes and interests change.

"Who are the most avid collectors of antiques—men or women?" I recently asked a dealer.

"The women usually begin it," he said, "but once the husbands are bitten by the bug they get the disease worse than their wives."

People collect the oddest things. One can understand a person collecting bottles, but one man who has a great array prizes them for their contents. He is a collector of rivers and has samples of the waters of the world's most famous streams carefully bottled and arranged alphabetically, from the Amazon to the Zambezi.

A more colorful collection which I have seen consists of hundreds of miniature bottles of liquor. Ranged in rows on specially built shelves, the bottles, with their divers shapes and different-colored liquids and labels, give the illusion of a stained-glass window. A person addicted to following a color scheme in his drinking could find here the appropriate hue for any mood.

The passion for collecting has been extended to all kinds of common and uncommon things. I have known New Englanders who have collected hourglasses, shaving mugs, tavern signs, compasses, fans, sets of chessmen, pistols, pipes, iron trivets, door knockers, weathervanes, bellows, caddy spoons, glass hats, china cats, dolls, telescopes, mirrors, pictures of Adam and Eve, bookplates, clocks, flasks, cologne bottles, inkstands, china and glass slippers and boots, little silver and enamel boxes, silhouettes, miniature books, paper weights, ivory and tortoise-shell paper cutters, snuffboxes, bells, butter molds, ship models, music boxes, buttons, and numerous other odds and ends which belonged to our ancestors.

At one time collecting pitchers was popular with women, one acquaintance of the writer having more than a hundred, some of them very beautiful, others grotesque, and still others unspeakably ugly. The collection was ruined when a shelf in the same cupboard collapsed under the weight of a large, heavy cut-glass punch bowl and came crashing down on the pitchers.

Yachtsmen, anglers, golfers, and others often collect things related to the sport in which they are interested. Doctors and lawyers frequently do the same according to their professions. Old books and prints dealing with a particular sport or profession are always worth collecting.

Doctors used to delight in decorating the walls of their waiting rooms with gruesome medical prints, a favorite one being Rembrandt's "The Anatomy Les-

The Romance of Collecting

son." Less disturbing was the Rogers' Group called "Going for the Doctor," which I remember standing on a marble-top walnut table in the bay window of the parlor of the doctor I used to go to in my youth. My present physician has a collection of old china teapots, including a pictorial one of the Boston Tea Party.

Doctors have always had unusual opportunities to pick up antiques because they get into people's houses, and in the past some members of the profession have assembled notable collections acquired mostly from their patients. Perhaps an old lady worried by the size of the medical bill she is running up will be told by her doctor to think nothing of it, as he will be glad to accept a certain old table or chair or mirror he has happened to notice in payment, and the patient gratefully accepts his offer. It is not suggested that such transactions are unfair or that the doctor takes advantage of his patient; but one is bound to observe that there have been cases in which the doctor has found himself in possession of a rare piece worth many times the amount of his bill. One doctor I knew did not even bother to bargain with a patient. He simply walked off with anything he saw that struck his fancy. If the matter was mentioned later, he laughed it off, or explained that he had merely borrowed the heirloom to photograph it and had forgotten to return it. But seldom did the patient get his property back.

Everybody knows the type of collector who is concerned with only one kind of antique and fills his house with examples of it. The best illustration is the clock collector, to whom there is no music like the slow and stately ticking of a company of ancient clocks. He knows the voice of each as first one and then another begins to strike the hour. But the majority of persons who are interested in antiques do not concentrate on any one thing; they have tastes that cover a wide field. Some, of course, are quite indiscriminate, but many more look for representative pieces which fit into their homes, and are never afraid to weed out as they discover new and better things. If they are looking for a table, a mirror, or an occasional chair to complete the furnishing of a room, they are always delighted when in the course of their search they come across an unusual piece of old glass, silver, or pewter. Naturally there are many collectors whose buying is drastically restricted by the size of their wallets. Every purchase has to be carefully considered, quite possibly even made at some personal sacrifice; but this makes for wise discrimination and adds to the pleasure of possession.

There is a distinction between being a collector and the owner of a collection. Years ago Edith Wharton wrote a story about a man in whom the collecting instinct was deeply implanted. There was a certain collection, the property of a man incapable of appreciating it fully, which he longed to possess, but he lacked the money to buy it. At length, the poor connoisseur found himself relatively rich. But acquisition of the collection failed to bring him the satisfaction he had anticipated and presently it was put up for sale and dispersed. Then the dealers began to notice that he was quietly buying back various items wherever he could find them. This continued over the years until in the end we see the col-

The Romance of Collecting

lector a poor man again, but happy in the possession of his antiques. By buying the collection in one swoop he deprived himself of the pleasures of the chase. He could not gloat over the quarry. Pride of discovery is as dominant an emotion of the true collector as pride of possession.

There are many people, of course, who have no use for antiques. They dislike the idea of putting old wine in new bottles, so to speak, and will have none of it around. Excessive love of antiques they consider a species of intellectual idol worship, and the fashion for old things a contradiction of the age in which we live. Their own fixation is for strictly modern furniture, and as members of a cult they are intolerant of anything else. Yet the style which they admire was anticipated a century or more ago by the craftsmen in the Shaker communities of New England and elsewhere, who created furniture as plain, severe, and functional as any to be seen today. And it was not machine-made or mass-produced either.

Our ancestors were really fortunate. They lived among things which were made for them by hand by master craftsmen who were not hurried but could work carefully, putting their souls into the task. In whatever medium they worked, the New England craftsmen were never unduly ambitious. Their productions were largely simple and natural, restrained in manner and taste. The straightforwardness and honesty of their workmanship, its grace and excellence, gives pleasure today to owners of their work.

New England is the oldest civilized section of the

United States. Its people were the first to establish themselves permanently. Because it is an old place where people have lived a long time, it naturally has a strong attraction for people interested in the past. To the collector of antiques it holds a special appeal as a region from which many characteristically American things have come and where many treasures of the old days may still be found.

2

Old Curiosity Shops and Antique Dealers

"YES," said the dealer, "our windfalls are of various kinds. Some customers are ignorant, and then I touch a dividend on my superior knowledge. Some are dishonest," and here he held up the candle, so that the light fell strongly on his visitor, "and in that case," he continued, "I profit by my virtue."

Those are the opening lines of Robert Louis Stevenson's short story "Markheim," which, it will be recalled, is about an antique dealer who is murdered in his shop. Although written in 1884, the description of the dealer's place of business in London would fit many antique shops to be seen in New England today. The dark, cavelike interior, crowded with a miscellaneous collection of clocks, mirrors, pictures, china, glassware, incongruous furniture, and curiosities of all kinds, is characteristic of a certain type of shop familiar to everybody.

Back-street places of this kind have always had a fascination for collectors, who never tire of exploring them in the hope of making a find.

The window of an antique shop adds interest to any street. Its profusion of things mirroring a world that is dead and gone is an invitation to adventure. There is hardly one that does not embody at least half a dozen chapters of history worth more than a passing glance. The mere sight of such a window is enough to arouse the hunting instinct in most of us.

Many antique shops were originally nothing but secondhand stores dealing in used furniture and other household goods and were gradually changed over as the dealer saw the possibilities in antiques. One dealer informed me that he learned his first lesson while working in his father's secondhand furniture store. One day a dealer in antiques offered him twenty-five dollars for a drop-leaf table he had bought for a dollar and a half. He refused the offer and began to look into the antique trade. A second dealer offered him forty dollars, but he turned this down, too, finally selling the table to a third dealer for fifty dollars. Shortly afterward he picked up for two dollars a pewter Communion service consisting of a tankard and two plates and two beakers which he sold for twelve dollars. His eyes were opened, and when soon after this his father died he transformed the secondhand store into an antique shop.

Cabinetmakers also drifted into the business. Called on to restore and refinish antique pieces, they began to pick up old furniture on their own account, which, after reconditioning, they sold, and before they knew it

Old Curiosity Shops and Antique Dealers

they had become full-fledged antique dealers. Others gained an insight into the trade by working as cabinet-makers for dealers who were not craftsmen themselves. Their knowledge of woods and workmanship stood them in good stead. They could tell instantly whether or not a piece had been touched.

"Sycamore, birch, and butternut are hard to tell apart," said one of them. "Fifty per cent of what is labeled CHERRY in museums is sycamore."

Many of the New England dealers are just natural-born Yankee traders who enjoy dealing in the miscellaneous things of the antique trade. It has been observed that some of these dealers in curiosities are themselves curiosities, but whether this is a cause or an effect of the dealing it is difficult to say. Certainly some of the collectors they do business with are eccentric. In any case, most of the Yankee dealers are gifted with the ability to buy as well as the ability to sell.

Some people who begin by pursuing antiques as a hobby become so interested that they drop everything else and are not happy until they establish themselves as dealers in shops of their own. Many women who are omnivorous collectors acquire so many antiques they don't know what to do with them and end by opening shops. At first it is just a hobby with them, but before long they become serious dealers. Dealing in antiques can run in the blood of a family. A number of New England antique businesses are now carried on by the third generation.

At first the inexperienced dealer, like the inexperienced collector, is liable to make mistakes. But he soon learns his business and is generally willing to admit that much of his knowledge was acquired by talking with customers. From different ones he picks up information about various lines of collecting which is extremely valuable. And once he learns his job he is glad to help the beginning collector with information and advice.

Every antique has a story to tell and the experienced dealer can read an old piece like a book. People are invariably curious as to where antiques come from. "Where on earth did you get that?" they ask, pointing at something which has attracted their interest. One Connecticut dealer had the same answer for everything, whether it was a bedstead, a bootjack, or one of those covered metal spittoons in the form of a tortoise which, if you step on its head, graciously opens up by raising its back shell. "Oh, I got that from a little old lady in Moodus," the dealer always answered.

Where do dealers find the antiques to keep their shops stocked? A large percentage of the business of any dealer is done with other dealers. Every shop has customers interested in certain categories of antiques and to meet their requirements the dealer picks up articles from other shops. City dealers constantly visit country dealers. The small-town dealer frequently knows of antiques which he could buy if he had the money, and the more affluent city dealer will pay him a commission for putting him in touch with the owners. The late Wallace Nutting frequently took advantage of tips given to him by local dealers and often succeeded in persuading persons to part with heirlooms which others had tried in vain to pry loose.

Old Curiosity Shops and Antique Dealers

Dealers also obtain things through the medium of small newspaper advertisements, by attending auctions, and by employing "pickers." A picker goes from house to house with a small truck or station wagon buying whatever he can. He usually operates in and around historic towns, sometimes working the same area for several seasons. Knocking at the door of a dwelling he asks the housewife if she has a spinning wheel she would like to sell, apparently on the theory that if there is one in the house it is probably broken and in the attic, which is the place where the dealer is most anxious to look around. The approach of one expert I know, when he is out picking, is to say, "Good morning, madam. I am not selling anything. I am buying. Have you anything in the attic you don't want?"

This dealer saw a clock in the kitchen of a house at which he called and offered to buy it, but the woman said the clock was her husband's and she could not sell it. The dealer returned later when the husband was at home and again offered to purchase the clock.

"Not for sale," said the man curtly.

There were five small children in the kitchen at the time, eating their supper, and in the hand of each the dealer placed a five-dollar bill. He waited a moment for the effect of this to sink in, and then, "What do you say?" he asked the father.

The man glanced up at the clock, then around at the children holding the money. "I guess you win," he said.

When the dealer returned to his shop a customer was waiting to see what he had picked up and was immediately interested in the clock.

"I knew it was a good clock," said the dealer, "but I didn't know how good. I put an arbitrary figure of five hundred dollars on it. The customer was as ignorant as I was about its value. He protested strongly at the price, but he was game and finally bought it. It was a gamble for both of us. Later we learned that the clock was a rare one worth fifteen hundred dollars."

The picking nowadays is not so good as it was. A dealer who used to keep three trucks busy combing the countryside says that a week's search now would not yield antiques enough to load a station wagon. Supplies were cut into so heavily during the boom days of the twenties that there is not much left of stocks that were limited in the first place. It is sometimes forgotten that a century or more ago there were far fewer people in New England than there are today. Lots of furniture which the dealer would now be glad to have was during the golden years taken out to the dump and discarded because it was not worth bothering with. Marble-top tables, sofas, side chairs, parlor suites, all the credentials of the well-appointed home of the last decades of the last century were abandoned, as people would not give them a second glance. One now sees more of this late Victorian furniture and other not-so-old antiques because of the relative scarcity of the better kind of really old items.

Many collectors profess affection for things of this late period which they know to be hideous or absurd, but the sentimental associations of some things are so strong that they discover in them beauties all their own, and from regarding them at first as simply amusing, they

Old Curiosity Shops and Antique Dealers

presently begin to fancy they are beautiful. This confusion of thought is perhaps a pardonable weakness and certainly from the dealer's standpoint fortunate.

But it must not be concluded from what has been said that there are no desirable antiques to be had. There are still many fine things of their kind in all lines in the shops. Even the most fastidious collector, who is never satisfied with the second-best, is tempted by what he sees, and for the modest collector there is an endless variety from which to choose. Difficult as the task is for the dealer, he nevertheless manages to keep up his stock. People die whose heirs care nothing for the antiques which are left. Others move from large houses to smaller ones or into apartments and have to get rid of many of their things. In these and other ways supplies keep coming into the market.

Fashions in collecting alter from decade to decade, reflecting the social changes of the times. To see what is happening one has only to notice what the antique shops have and have not for sale. Large houses and the massive pieces of furniture that were made for them have no place today. Smaller homes require furnishings on a diminished scale. A man who recently moved from the big old house in which he had lived all his life into a smaller, more modern place found there was not room enough in his new dining room for the large ancestral sideboard he had brought with him, nor were the ceilings of sufficient height to accommodate his ancient tall clock. The size of the house made it impossible for him to hang the large oil paintings which had adorned his former abode. The vogue today is of necessity for small pieces of furniture, small pictures, and small accessories of all kinds.

Of course, the dealer gets more for those objects on which the spotlight of popular favor happens to be momentarily focused than he does for the things which have not caught the passing fancy of the crowd. In every shop there are neglected treasures of beauty and value to which the wise collector, ignoring the current vogue, turns his attention, because a good thing always remains so, regardless of whether it is sought after or not. The collector who follows his own instincts and personal inclinations probably fares better in the long run than the person who merely follows the popular trend.

Even dealers have their own preferences and are often collectors themselves. Several times I have inquired the price of things in antique shops, only to be told they were not for sale, as the dealer has a special fancy for such things himself and will pay me a good price for anything of the kind. But usually the dealer who is also a collector has duplicates he is willing to sell. Often he succeeds in imparting his enthusiasm for certain objects to his customers and starts them collecting along the same line. Dealers have been responsible for more than one antique fad.

There are regions within regions even in New England and every dealer worth his salt caters to local pride and prejudice by specializing in things which have local associations. What Maine person, for example, particularly one living in Augusta, would not be glad to have

Old Curiosity Shops and Antique Dealers 37

above almost any other clock one by Frederic Wingate, the Augusta clockmaker mentioned in the preceding chapter. The work of a local silversmith, or pewterer, or other craftsman is generally highly regarded in the area where he worked. Old prints and paintings depicting local views and books dealing with the town in which the dealer has his shop are usually in steady demand, and, owing to the local interest in them, bring good prices.

Not all antiques which turn up in New England are of native origin. Dealers have ranged far afield in their search for things, and in years gone by many New Englanders who went abroad brought home small objects as souvenirs of their European sojourns. Some even made extensive purchases of antique furniture. Foreign dealers reaped a rich harvest. During the nineteen-twenties a business called "bird nesting" flourished in France. Americans were taken on treasure hunts through the French countryside by dealers who had planted items in old cottages, caretakers' lodges, and disused chateaux. There is no doubt that antiques show to the best advantage in appropriate surroundings, and the unwary tourist who bought a nondescript chair or table in a humble farmhouse kitchen, or a questionable clock in the hall of a grand house, paid handsomely for the privilege of buying it in the right atmosphere. There were women as well as men bird nesters, some of them expatriate Americans who preyed on their fellow countrymen.

Genuine antiques bought abroad may be brought into this country duty free if they are a hundred years old;

but many an American collector has found that, even when he can show the dealer's invoice stating that the articles are at least a century old, the United States Customs officials have taken a different view and made him pay duty because the things were actually not so old as they were represented to be.

AUCTIONEER

3

Going Going Gone: Town and Country Auctions

AUCTIONS in town and country have been popular in New England for centuries. These sales, or "vendues," as they were called, used to be announced by the town crier, or by the distribution of handbills, or by newspaper advertisements. Sometimes all three methods were employed to give notice of the same sale. These methods are still used today, but the function of the town crier is now largely fulfilled by the radio announcer.

Auctions were frequently held at the local tavern, which was not merely a place of entertainment, but a center where public and private business was transacted. Sometimes an auctioneer provided refreshment for the crowd. If the bidding lagged, he held up a bottle, offering a drink to the next bidder. Someone would raise the bid a cent and be the envy of all as he took a swig.

Peddlers held vendues at fairs, musters, and other special gatherings where the people turned out in force. In his *American Notes*, Nathaniel Hawthorne describes the peddlers at Williams College on commencement day in 1838.

> The most characteristic part of the scene [he says] was where the peddlers, ginger-bread sellers, etc., were collected. There was a peddler there from New York State who sold his wares by auction, and I could have stood and listened to him all day long. Sometimes he would put up a heterogeny of articles in a lot—as a paper of pins, a lead pencil, and a shaving box—and knock them all down, perhaps for ninepence. Bunches of lead pencils, steel pens, pound cakes of shaving soap, gilt finger-rings, bracelets, clasps and other jewellery, cards of pearl buttons, or steel, bundles of wooden combs, boxes of matches, suspenders and, in short, everything—dipping his hand down into his wares, with the promise of a wonderful lot, and producing, perhaps, a bottle of opodeldoc, and joining it with a lead pencil.

Hawthorne would perhaps have been interested in the luck of a person who at a country auction in Maine a few years ago purchased a bean pot and its contents for small change. In the bean pot was discovered the rare first edition of Hawthorne's *Fanshawe*, a book worth over a thousand dollars.

There also turned up in Maine the rarest and most sought after of American literary treasures. This was a copy of Poe's *Tamerlane and Other Poems*, of which scarcely a dozen copies are known. One in good condi-

Going Going Gone: Town and Country Auctions

tion has sold for as much as $31,000. This book, which is really not a book at all but a small forty-page pamphlet, has a romantic, if rather baffling, history. It was printed in Boston in 1827 by a young printer named Calvin F. S. Thomas, who is thought to have been a friend of Poe's. Poe was eighteen at the time and it was his first literary work. His name does not appear on the pamphlet. On the title page it is stated that the poems are "By a Bostonian," but though born in Boston, Poe was not a proper Bostonian. He had enlisted in the Army at Boston under the name of Edgard A. Perry, after quarreling with his guardian, John Allen, in Richmond. When the late Charles Eliot Norton of Harvard was asked whether he did not think Poe's writings had in them the glory of Greece and the grandeur of Rome, he replied, "Yes, and the degradation of Baltimore."

The circumstances surrounding the publication of *Tamerlane* are largely conjectural. It is believed that Poe agreed to stand the expense of having his poems printed, but when the work was done was unable to pay Thomas, who disposed of the edition as wastepaper, except for a few copies which he had given to Poe, perhaps for the purpose of soliciting orders, or for presenting to reviewers. Nobody knows how many copies were printed, but the edition was undoubtedly small. Poe included revised versions of the poems in *Tamerlane* in another collection called *Al Aaraaf*, published two years later in Baltimore. In this second pamphlet he acknowledged the printing of *Tamerlane* in 1827, but claimed it had been "suppressed through circumstances of a private nature."

The public at large did not become aware of the value of *Tamerlane* until an article on rare books by Vincent Starrett called "Have You a Tamerlane in Your Attic?" was published in the *Saturday Evening Post* in 1925. An elderly woman living with her sister in an attic in Worcester read the article, but was uncertain whether the *Tamerlane* she had was the sort which Mr. Starrett said was worth $10,000. But she got in touch with Charles A. Goodspeed, the famous Boston bookseller, who found the buff-colored pamphlet to be genuine. He sold it to Owen D. Young for $17,500, and gave the Worcester woman a check for $14,000. This particular copy is now owned by the New York Public Library. Six of the eleven known copies are in institutions.

The eleventh copy, which was discovered in Skowhegan, Maine, was a miserable specimen which brought a record low of $4300 when it was sold at auction in New York at the American Art Association Anderson Galleries in December, 1938. Its earliest known owner was a Skowhegan carpenter and builder named Joseph Bigelow. But no matter how poor the copy, if you are able to secure at a country auction of antiques an insignificant pamphlet in printed wrappers entitled TAMERLANE AND OTHER POEMS. BY A BOSTONIAN. . . . *Boston: Calvin F. S. Thomas . . . Printer. 1827*, with two lines quoted from Cowper between the "Bostonian" and the "Boston," you have the rarest of American first editions. The quotation which Poe used on the cover of his teen-age work was singularly appropriate:

> Young heads are giddy, and young hearts are warm,
> And make mistakes for manhood to reform.

Going Going Gone: Town and Country Auctions

Frequenters of city sales rooms in which pictures, rare books, manuscripts, prints, old silver, antique furniture, and other artistic and literary valuables are auctioned watch the trend of prices closely to see whether new heights are reached or there are losses on previous values. Many ups and downs can be accounted for by changes of fashion in collecting. Of course, if you follow the current vogue, you pay more than if you pursue a less popular line of collecting. Important things often show heavy losses on earlier values because they come up for resale only a few years after they were bought at a high price. When this occurs such things seldom do well, as there is a feeling that the person who wishes to dispose of something so soon after purchasing it may have regretted buying it in the first place. Then, too, the owner may be the person who because of his interest in a particular kind of antique is the one who has been chiefly responsible for establishing the market value, and when he changes from buyer to seller a fall in prices almost invariably follows. The artistic merit of a thing, however, does not change with the value, and lower prices may enable appreciative persons to make acquisitions they could not afford before.

Some people take a melancholy view of auctions, seeing in the sale of the contents of an old house in the country a note of valediction and doom. They picture the owners, perhaps an aged and infirm couple, forced to sell the old homestead and all their belongings. Poverty and death often are the causes of these sales, but appearances are sometimes misleading. During the summer city dealers sometimes travel about the countryside with loads of furniture and, hiring the barn and grounds of some nice old place, will auction the furniture off to summer residents and others. Local dealers frequently do the same thing, bringing stuff from isolated places to towns, where it is easier to get a crowd. An auction is not necessarily a preface to poverty. A person may simply be moving elsewhere and wish to get rid of a lot of old junk he cannot take with him.

New Englanders are a saving people, sometimes accumulating and hoarding things to the point of eccentricity, and you never can tell what will come up for sale at an auction. Here, for example, is a list of articles sold by auction after the death of Harry Crocker, and his wife, in Nantucket, copied from the list published at the time of the sale and preserved in the notebook of Mrs. Frederick Mason Stone, who was born in 1828 and spent her girlhood on Nantucket Island. The Crockers lived near the North Shore in a house long since removed or taken down. "They had no children," says Mrs. Stone, "kept no boarders, never entertained company, and lived in a small house." Yet, incredible as it may appear, they possessed the following things:

150 chairs	50 glass lamps
50 covered tubs	350 baskets
42 chamber toilets	21 blankets
3 dining sets	42 night caps
14 mouse traps	9 mattresses
13 bureaus	115 dresses
19 coal hods	155 night gowns
16 bird cages	6 pounds spool cotton

Going Going Gone: Town and Country Auctions

There were other miscellaneous items, including toweling enough to last the heirs a lifetime.

There are eccentric buyers as well as eccentric sellers at New England auctions. One newspaper editor who is an auction addict revels in buying the oddest and most useless objects imaginable. He comes home with the craziest collection of things which neither he nor anyone else could possibly find any use for, but absurd or hideous as they may be, he professes a profound affection for them, and it amuses him to buy them.

For many people the fascination of an auction does not lie so much in the articles offered for sale, or the crowd present, or the place where the auction is held, as it does in the auctioneer himself. People love to hear a good auctioneer in action, and it must be admitted that many of them are masters of the art of advocacy. They know how to arrest and hold the attention of a crowd. They know how to coax and cajole and keep the bidding going at a lively pace. They know how to play off one contender against another. They can spin a web of words around a commonplace object so that it seems the most desirable thing in the world. They are able to get the last penny for it, too. Occasionally, they let something go cheaply to maintain interest. Courteous, good-humored, and amusing, they nevertheless know the right moment to scold their hearers. This is seemingly one of the traditions of the calling, but it takes an experienced auctioneer to know how and when to do it properly.

Once at a sale of antiques in the house of a deceased Connecticut millionaire at which I was a bystander the customary berating was particularly ill-timed and badly done. The sale was such an important one that a cry of New York auctioneers had been imported to conduct it. It was a long sale and after luncheon a relief auctioneer took over. He was young, quite Hollywoodish in appearance, and somewhere had acquired what sometimes passes for a cultured accent. The fellow didn't do so badly at first, but he had only been selling a short time before he decided to go into his scolding act. He felt very, very hurt, he said, at the discourtesy of the audience in not paying strict attention to him. There was buzzing, he declared, and he went on to chide the people as if they were a lot of bad-mannered and ill-bred children. The whole thing was poorly timed and what he said in worse taste, but carried away by his own bad art he went on and on to the discomfort of everybody, until at length the situation was relieved by a cynical gentleman in tweeds exclaiming, "Fiddlesticks, Professor!" at which the crowd laughed and the youthful auctioneer was hurriedly deposed by his colleagues.

An auctioneer is the agent of the owner and is bound by his instructions. He cannot bid himself and he must use reasonable diligence in the conduct of a sale, the terms of which must be stated at the outset. He must not be guilty of misdescribing the goods, as that is fraud. An old-time trick of the unscrupulous auctioneer is to pretend to receive bids which are not in fact made. It is also fraudulent to use by-bidders or confederates to run up prices. But the law relating to auctions is rarely invoked, and there is no doubt that some auctioneers employ persons to stimulate the zeal of legitimate bidders.

Going Going Gone: Town and Country Auctions 49

Only once, however, have I known an auction to be broken up. The auctioneer stopped the sale immediately when a person present charged him with unfairness. He was a barnstormer holding a summer sale of antiques in an old coast town. He had hired a hall, and the moment his methods were challenged he declared the sale adjourned and ordered the lights put out. The people present were furious at the man who stopped the show.

The Uniform Sales Act, which has been adopted by most States, contains the following provisions covering sales by auction:

> Section 21. In the case of sale by auction—(1). Where goods are put up for sale by auction in lots, each lot is the subject of a separate contract of sale.
>
> (2.) A sale by auction is complete when the auctioneer announces its completion by the fall of the hammer, or in other customary manner. Until such announcement is made, any bidder may retract his bid; and the auctioneer may withdraw the goods from sale unless the auction has been announced to be without reserve.
>
> (3.) A right to bid may be reserved expressly by or on behalf of the seller.
>
> (4.) Where notice has not been given that a sale by auction is subject to a right to bid on behalf of the seller, it shall not be lawful for the seller to bid himself or to employ or induce any person to bid at such sale on his behalf, or for the auctioneer to employ or induce any person to bid at such sale on his behalf, or for the auctioneer to employ or induce any person to bid at such sale on behalf of the seller or knowingly to take any bid from the seller or any person employed

by him. Any sale contravening this rule may be treated as fraudulent by the buyer.

The custom of hanging out a red flag at an auction is a very old one, dating back to Roman days, when the spoils of war were disposed of at public sale. A spear was used as the sign of an auction. Soon a red flag was added, and this continued to be the emblem of the auctioneer even after this special mode of sale had been extended to property in general. Ever since, the red flag and spear, or rather flagstaff, symbols of blood and war, have been used for this same purpose.

It is difficult to lay down any rules for the person who attends New England antique auctions, but here are a few points which are perhaps worth noting.

One, you have to know the auctioneer, which includes knowing his by-bidders, if he uses them. If you are really friendly with him, regarded by him as one of his following, so to speak, you get favored treatment.

Two, with an honest auctioneer who works without by-bidders a private citizen can nearly always outbid a dealer for anything he really wants. Lots of people just sit back in exasperation when a dealer starts bidding, whereas a moment's thought will show that the dealer has to stop short of what he will charge for an article in his shop. I know one or two high-class dealers who will go within ten dollars of their expected retail price on a hundred-dollar item, but normally a dealer expects to double his money, which leaves plenty of leeway for a private buyer to make a saving. Furthermore, if you cultivate the friendship of dealers, they hesitate to run up a good customer.

Going Going Gone: Town and Country Auctions

Three, pay no attention to the trimmings, such as "contents of old house in the same family two hundred years." The only thing that counts is the merchandise itself. You have to know a good piece when you see it, and you have to know, not necessarily what it is worth, but what it is worth to you. You must also know your own particular failing at auctions. Some people get caught in the spirit of competition, and cannot let go even when they don't want the stuff; others get feeling poor halfway through, and lose things because they won't toss in the last two dollars and a half that would take it. Also it is probably a mistake to pass a "steal" because you are saving your money for something else you want; two to one the latter will go out of sight.

One hears it said that the days are gone when bargains were to be had at auctions. This is not true. There are just as many bargains and the voice of the auctioneer is heard as frequently as ever in New England.

"A fine, genuine old piece, ladies and gentlemen, a hundred years old, as good as the day it was made and a rare example. What am I offered for this heirloom? Will somebody start it off at ten dollars? Anybody give ten dollars? What do I hear, five dollars? I have five dollars for it. Who says six? Thank you, madam. I have six dollars. Going for six dollars . . ."

Recently, at the end of a country sale, the auctioneer as a final gesture sacrificed for a dollar and a quarter the kitchen table which the clerk of the auction had used to keep a record of the sales. After the buyer had driven off with it, the discovery was made that the entire cash proceeds of the auction were in the table drawer.

The LAWYER

4

Reproductions, Fakes, and Thefts

THERE is something to be said for reproductions. Not those which are made with the intention of deceiving, but the straightforward copies made by master craftsmen which are honestly sold. The stock of antiques is limited and is decreasing steadily every year as a result of damage and destruction. At the same time, the demand has been increasing, until it has reached a point where there are not enough old pieces to go round. A reproduction lacks, of course, the aura and distinction which time alone can impart, nor does it have the historical associations which antiques often possess, but in the case of old furniture beauty is largely a matter of form and design and if you can get these, you have a good thing, regardless of when a piece was made.

Often the original is unique and the only hope one has of ever possessing anything like it is to have it copied. A person who lives with antiques may need a particular piece of furniture and unable to afford the genuine article will use a reproduction rather than go without it.

There are still cabinetmakers with their own shops who are as expert as any of the old-time craftsmen and still do almost everything by hand, just as it used to be done. An expert cabinetmaker I knew specialized in Chippendale mirrors which were perfectly made and finished. The ornamental gilt leaves at the top and down the sides were whittled out of wood instead of being molded in plaster. A person needing such a mirror for decorative purposes, but unable to buy an original, was surely justified in taking the copy.

A notable family of master craftsmen are the Margolies family of Hartford. They have been cabinetmakers for at least four generations. The late Nathan Margolies, who founded the business in Hartford, served his apprenticeship in England. He made many reproductions of family pieces to order—tables, chairs, etc.—and also a good deal of documentary furniture, including the Connecticut sunflower chest, the Savery lowboy and highboy, and the Washington Inaugural sofa and the flat-topped Washington desk with the fake drawers on one side in the City Hall, New York. A set of twelve Connecticut Senate chairs was made for the Aetna Life Insurance Company from the original, in the collection of Morgan B. Brainard. More recently Harold Margolies, who now carries on the business, supplied the furniture for the governor's mansion in Hartford. Many of the designs used by this family of cabinetmakers during the past fifty years were copied from the Pendleton

Reproductions, Fakes, and Thefts

Collection in the Rhode Island School for Design at Providence.

Mention of Washington is a reminder that recently in the home of a New England antique dealer I noticed a pair of Washington andirons. They were about the size of the frequently reproduced Hessian-soldier ones. The twin full-length figures of the first President show him wearing the decoration of the Order of the Cincinnati. Had they been genuine they would have been about a hundred and fifty years old, but they were reproductions. They had come from the estate of an antique dealer who had had a dozen pairs made.

A piece of furniture may be so extensively restored that it is actually more of a reproduction than an antique. The experienced collector never buys anything unless it is in its original state. If repairs are necessary, he has the work done himself. In this way he knows exactly to what extent a piece has been restored. There are, of course, collectors who consider it an act of vandalism to do any restoring at all. They want their antiques to remain in a virginal state, even if they are rickety, or perhaps lacking a part. They take the attitude that it is better to have an antique ruined by time than by the hand of the restorer. But most people buy antiques for practical use as well as for the aesthetic pleasure they derive from them, and are not averse to having their old furniture restored and strengthened.

It might be supposed that the many stories of antique faking would discourage collectors, but it seems to work the other way, people apparently reasoning that if the field of antiques is one the fakers find worth cultivating, it must be worth the attention of decent folk. Knowing there are shams on the market is a challenge that adds zest to the collecting game. It places a premium on knowledge. Some people, by experience, seem to acquire a special sense which enables them to scent a spurious production a long way off. Yet even the experts are sometimes fooled and good dealers defrauded.

Wallace Nutting, who manufactured a line of reproductions of colonial furniture in an old hat factory in Framingham, Massachusetts, once told me that he burned his name into all the furniture he made after he found that one of his pieces had been deceptively aged and passed off on a great art museum as a genuine antique. With the lapse of time, this Framingham furniture will itself become ancient and timeworn, and since it was well made from authentic models, it will perhaps be in special request. When that time comes, probably current copies will appear branded with Wallace Nutting's name.

One of his reproductions I used to age myself. When I had a book shop in an old brick house in Hartford, I bought from him two signboards, copied from an antique New England tavern sign, and had them both painted and lettered. As I thought a somewhat faded sign was more in keeping with the place than a freshly painted one and would give the impression of a long-established business, I let one sign weather out of sight on the roof, until the other, hanging over the doorway, had become almost illegible and had to be repainted. I then replaced it with the sign that had been aging on the housetop. In this way I always had a sign of the right vintage.

Reproductions, Fakes, and Thefts

Many antiques are assembled from parts of other antiques. If the work is well done by one with a thorough technical knowledge, it is difficult to detect the fraud. Take old clocks, for example. The dials of one maker may be fitted to the movements of another and housed in a case of unidentified name and origin. Sometimes the names on the dials of old clocks are forgeries, and repairers of clocks in the old days thought nothing of signing those on which they had worked. Not much reliance can be placed on the label found inside the case as a clue to the maker of the clock, because the works were often sold separately, the purchaser having the case made by a local cabinetmaker.

It is the rarer types of clocks, like the "grandmother" clock and the "banjo" clock, which have attracted the attention of the fakers, because they bring more money. The grandmother is, of course, a diminutive version of the tall-case grandfather clock. A grandfather may be seven or eight feet tall, but a grandmother is never much more than five feet high, and may measure as little as three feet. Obviously the easiest way to make a fake grandmother clock is to cut down the case of a grandfather, though the clock chosen to be operated on has to be selected with care. A grandfather clock with a large hood and dial will appear all out of proportion if the height of the case is reduced. It will look like a gnome with a monstrous head. So the clever faker searches for a tall clock with a small dial, and either cuts down the old case or makes a new one, which he then ages.

It is not so easy to fake a banjo clock. It takes an expert to do it successfully. But many banjo clocks have been sold as genuinely old which in reality were nothing but skillful reconstructions. With knowledge of the scarcer types of these clocks, the gifted faker can make a rare example out of an ordinary banjo, complete with brass finial eagle and interesting glass-panel painting. Even dealers have sometimes been hoodwinked by these creations.

In some of the books on clockmaking the name of David Aird appears among the list of clockmakers, but he was a thief who merely pretended to be a clockmaker. In 1785 he advertised himself, in Middletown, Connecticut, as a clock- and watchmaker from London, and after gathering a lot of timepieces absconded with them. A year or so later he had the effrontery to return to Middletown and steal a couple of china-faced watches from a Middletown resident. Aird was a horse thief as well as a clock thief, and for the former offense was whipped and made to ride the wooden horse in Hartford.

Old pieces of furniture can be completely changed and sometimes two antiques can be made to appear where there was only one before. The bottom of a highboy may be made into a lowboy, the top into a desk. From the wreckage of several pieces it is frequently possible to salvage enough parts to assemble a new piece. Tables are often constructed from two or three broken ones. All the parts are genuinely old, but the resulting piece is not an antique in the sense understood by a collector. Furniture made up in this way is more difficult to detect than the wholly new fake.

A common fake of this kind is the antique sofa built

Reproductions, Fakes, and Thefts

around four old legs. If you examine the bottoms of the legs for fresh telltale saw marks, none will be visible because they came from an old piece of furniture. Perhaps the maker picked up a dilapidated table with square grooved legs which he could use. Old wood, of course, is employed for the frame.

New fabrics on sofas and chairs can be aged by immersion in faintly colored liquid, though some prefer to spray the tint on with an atomizer. It is also easy to fade textiles artificially. Old tapestries are often repaired and retouched, but this, like the restoration of pictures, is not faking.

Much artifice goes into making new furniture old, though the business is not so extensive at present as might be supposed. Yet the temptation to manufacture fakes is bound to increase as real antiques become harder to find and values advance. I have always doubted the story of the worm holes made with a charge of birdshot, but I do not doubt that they have been added with a tool. New pieces are roughly treated to wear off the edges. A particularly clumsy piece of faking is fairly usual in "aging" chairs. Natural use wears the front feet round as the chair is tipped and dragged forward. The fakers, unable to leave well enough alone, often take a rasp and round the edges of the back feet too, even the fronts of them. Such crude work does not fool the expert, but fakes are intended chiefly for the unwary and inexperienced buyer.

To give an old color to wood, it is sometimes burned with chemicals, or treated with permanganate of potash, or stained with walnut juice or other coloring matter.

One way used to impart an old finish is to apply a thin coat of benzine in which a little wax has been dissolved and then rub with steel wool. It is legitimate, of course, to use the aging process when a genuine old piece has been restored and it is necessary to bring the new portions into harmony with the old.

Tool marks are often an indication of the authenticity of an antique. When you see curved saw marks, for instance, on the bottom of a drawer, you know the piece is recent, because they come from a circular power saw; the older up-and-down saw left straight marks. Of course, the up-and-down saw continued in use long after the circular saw was invented, so, as usual, there is no conclusive proof of age, only of youth.

The hardware used may also betray a fake. Pointed screws, for example, were not made before the middle of the nineteenth century and their presence in a piece of furniture claimed to be older than that is a giveaway. Although machine-made screws began to be used about the time of the War of 1812, they were blunt-ended. Fakers are aware of this and in a cleverly made counterfeit will use the old pointless screws and hand-wrought nails. But by removing a screw it is sometimes possible to tell from the rust and the condition of the hole whether it has been embedded in the wood a long time or not. Since it is known at what periods certain types of knobs, brasses, and hinges were used, the hardware found on antique furniture, or the marks left by the original fittings, are useful in dating a piece.

It is possible in the case of furniture with large turnings—tip tables, for example—to determine whether a piece is modern or not by taking measurements. Old turnings which have seasoned for many years have shrunk unevenly and are never perfectly round. In the case of smaller turnings, however, the inequalities of age can be produced by soaking the wood before turning and drying it rapidly afterward, as it then contracts unevenly.

Smell may also play a part in establishing the validity of a piece. Like old houses, old furniture often has an unmistakable odor of oldness about it which modern pieces do not have. Nor apparently does this indication of age cling to the antique parts of an assembled piece. This aroma is most noticeable in what the furniture trade calls "case goods"—desks, bureaus, chests, cupboards, and cabinets. It is also present in old clocks. Almost any genuine old piece with doors or drawers is apt to have it, and thus far the fakers have not discovered a way to reproduce it. The drawers of old spice cabinets often smell of the spices once kept in them, but that is different, and such scents can be duplicated.

Sometimes, to meet a popular craze, an article will be reproduced wholesale. When the public became infatuated with glass paperweights containing tiny flowers and other designs in color, hundreds of thousands were made for the antique market, including some clever imitations from Japan and Czechoslovakia. People who had long collected these delightful glass objects and could tell by the look and feel of them that they were not genuine weren't fooled by these fakes, but many inexperienced persons bought the new ones and were probably as pleased with them as if they had been genuinely old.

Faked pedigrees often help to sell antiques. Dealers endowed with vivid imaginations can invent stories intended to spur on a customer for almost everything in their shops. Clever rogues some of them are, but after a while some of their stories have a familiar sound. "I got that from an old lady who inherited it from her grandmother. It has been in the same family for generations." It should be added that this was said of a palpable fake. "I tried for years to get this piece and had to pay practically what I am asking for it." And of another object, "A prominent collector who has had his eye on it is going to feel awfully sorry if he learns it has been sold." Of still another specimen, "I like it myself and hate to sell it because you don't see many of them nowadays." Whether the men or women dealers are the worse offenders is a moot question.

The advice usually given to beginners is to do business with reputable dealers only, at least until one has learned by study to tell good examples from bad, and gained sufficient experience to avoid most of the pitfalls. But part of the fascination of the pursuit is to visit all kinds of shops, from the unassuming junk shop in a city back street to the country barn in which even the haylofts are filled with old things. Despite all warnings, there is not a collector who has not at one time or another bought spurious antiques in the belief that they were genuine.

There are few branches of the antique trade that have

Reproductions, Fakes, and Thefts

not at one time or another been exploited by the counterfeiters. As soon as there is a demand in a certain field, the fakes begin to appear, many of them excellent imitations. It is easy, for example, to confer a look of age and venerability on pewter by reproducing the patina, and then mark it with the touch of some American maker whose work is being sought. Old unmarked pewter is frequently impressed with forged touches. Freshly marked pewter should always be regarded with suspicion, and one should make sure that a particular piece is something the pewterer whose touch it bears could have made and is not of later date. Pewter in the course of time becomes pitted and eroded, and while the fakers can give new pewter the old look, they have never succeeded in giving it the old feeling. The surface condition of the metal is the surest guide to its age.

It is also easy to give iron the appearance of antiquity. Mention has been made of the Washington andirons which a dealer had reproduced, and many other old styles have been duplicated, including the Hessian-soldier andirons. Old cast-iron hitching posts with horses' heads or in the form of a Negro boy holding a ring have been imitated. There are blacksmiths in New England who make a business of reproducing artistic old handwrought iron, such as doorknockers, foot scrapers, and all kinds of building and furniture hardware. There are also manufacturers of antique metalware reproductions in brass as well as iron. These are not made for the purpose of deceiving anyone, but since even the worn appearance of age is simulated, unscrupulous dealers sometimes claim that such reproductions are original and it must be owned it is sometimes difficult to tell whether they are or not. Old brass is apt to be a lighter color and not so reddish as modern brass, as it contained more zinc, with perhaps some tin, and less copper than is now used. If the style of hardware used on furniture is not appropriate to the period or the type of the particular piece, the claim that it is original is not true.

Museums and libraries have suffered from the depredations of thieves, who have carried away old paintings, prints, small *objets d'art*, and books. One of the most notorious thefts of this kind in New England occurred a few years ago, when a $50,000 Shakespeare folio was stolen from the library of Williams College. The ancient tome was taken by a thirty-six-year-old shoe salesman from Glens Falls, New York, who posed as a college professor to gain access to the library. Three Buffalo men had promised him $10,000 for taking the book, but he said that all he received was $200.

The robbery was carefully planned and the thief was coached in the part he was to play. He paid several visits to the Buffalo Public Library "to become acquainted with books."

"Then," said the shoe salesman, "with a forged letter from the president of Middlebury College to the president of Williams College—with my hair grayed and with ribboned Oxford glasses on—I introduced myself to the librarian of Williams College—it was a woman—as Professor Sinclair E. Gillingham."

When the librarian permitted him to use the folio for research, he substituted a dummy copy for the original.

Reproductions, Fakes, and Thefts

This was in February. Early in July the bogus professor and the three Buffalo men were arrested. Late in August the United States Attorney's office announced that the book, which was described as having a red gold-tooled morocco binding measuring nine by thirteen inches, had been recovered.

The disposal of excessively rare books and well-known pictures must present an almost insurmountable "fencing" problem for the thief. Stolen masterpieces are seldom anything but white elephants. Stealing them is a crime that definitely does not pay, unless the theft is commissioned in advance by a crazy collector whose possessive passion has been excited by some rarity. Such a possibility was suggested when Watteau's small masterpiece, "L'Indifferent," was stolen from the Louvre ten years ago. Here was a picture measuring only eight by ten inches valued at $100,000. It was a condensed fortune, a piece of concentrated perfection of a size which permitted continued concealment. Did some collector have an uncontrollable impulse to possess it? The suggestion was not altogether fantastic.

Manufacturing antique picture frames which show all the ravages of time is a business that has grown up in recent years. It is an honest trade. The frames are frankly sold as replicas. They are made because museums and private collectors find them better suited to old pictures than the heavy frames which were in vogue during the nineteenth century. Dealers have discovered that they help to sell old paintings.

The Caledonian Market in London used to be a favorite haunt of American collectors. This vast open-air secondhand mart is now closed, but in the far twenties it was a great attraction. I went there with an Irish artist, who was in quest of frames for his own pictures, and we came away with several old paintings, purchased solely for their frames.

One day in the back room of a bookshop in a New England city I saw a painting of a British man-of-war under full sail. There was no mistaking the vessel's nationality as she was flying the British Union Jack. The bookseller, who dealt in prints and an occasional painting as well as books, had just acquired it. I remarked on what an excellent piece of work it was.

"But it's too bad," I said, "it isn't an American ship. You could sell it quicker for more money."

Passing the dealer's shop a couple of weeks later, I noticed the picture in the window. It had undergone a remarkable change. By the simple altering of a square inch or two of the canvas the ship had been given a new character. Instead of the British flag, she was flying the Stars and Stripes.

One method used by print thieves who despoil rare books of their illustrations is to leave a string treated with acid between the leaves. By the time they return the acid has eaten the plate free, so it can be easily slipped out and smuggled away.

Book collectors who have rare books that are imperfect because a page or two happens to be missing have been known to take the leaves they lack from library or booksellers' copies. Synthetic first editions are sometimes assembled by unscrupulous booksellers, but only inexperienced bibliophiles fall for such fakes.

Reproductions, Fakes, and Thefts

The late Crompton T. Johnson, the rare-book dealer, who at one time had a bookshop in Farmington, Connecticut, missed several valuable old volumes from his collection. The books turned up in the hands of a leading New York bookseller, who, when Mr. Johnson claimed them, promptly turned the books over to him. A thief can pass no better title than he has, and even a bona fide purchaser for value acquires no title to stolen property as against the rightful owner. The New York dealer remembered purchasing the books from a prominent woman who was one of his customers. Although it was known that she sometimes visited Farmington, he did not believe that a person of her social standing could possibly be the thief and he never mentioned the matter to her.

It has been said, "Some steal for profit—they are criminals; some for pleasure—they are kleptomaniacs; others for pleasure and profit combined—they are collectors."

In March, 1948, a gang of thieves who for two years had been looting the homes of summer residents in Maine and Vermont of antiques and selling them in southern New England were rounded up in Auburn, Maine. They were held on a charge of stealing a grandfather clock worth one hundred and fifty dollars. Those arrested were Gordon A. Jones, his wife, her two brothers, and another man, all of Auburn. Among the Maine summer homes burglarized were those of former United States Secretary of Labor Frances Perkins and Dr. Donald Gates, a Massachusetts physician. The former had a valuable desk taken, the latter a highboy which had been in his family two hundred years. The police estimated that the thieves during the two years they were active stole antiques worth a hundred thousand dollars.

The gang operated only in the winter, using different methods of approach. If there was snow on the ground, they would take a circuitous route to the back door of a house, so their footsteps would not be visible from the road. At other times, they boldly drove a truck up to the front door and loaded it. Sometimes they lived for several days in a house while wrapping and packing china and glassware in boxes. They did not make a clean sweep of a place, but usually took only what looked good to them, a few things here, a few things there. Some houses were entered and nothing was touched. Their thefts were generally not discovered until months afterward, when the owners came to open their houses for the summer.

Some of the loot was disposed of in Massachusetts, but most of it to dealers in Connecticut, first in Manchester, and then in Hartford, Glastonbury, Clinton, East Haddam, Saybrook, Willimantic, Rocky Hill, and Windsor. Jones, who did the peddling, posed as a Christmas-tree agent from Maine. He also claimed he was a worker in a Connecticut factory and collected the antiques from his neighbors when he went home to Vermont week ends. Later he said he was an antique dealer with a large warehouse in Maine. Actually, Jones knew little about antiques or their value, and got only a tithe of what the things were worth, but his story seemed

Reproductions, Fakes, and Thefts

plausible to the dealers who bought the stolen goods. They often buy from freelance "pickers."

A great deal of the plunder was recovered by the State Police. Some of it was still in the antique shops, but most of it was in the hands of the persons to whom the dealers had sold it. In almost every instance they could remember those who had bought the things which they had acquired from Jones, and the police were thus able to trace the antiques into private homes all over Connecticut and part of Massachusetts. The dealers were, of course, the losers, as they had to refund the purchase price to their customers, but were themselves without recourse. A few dealers to whom Jones tried to sell declined to buy. Antiques by the truckload looked too good to be true. They were the lucky ones.

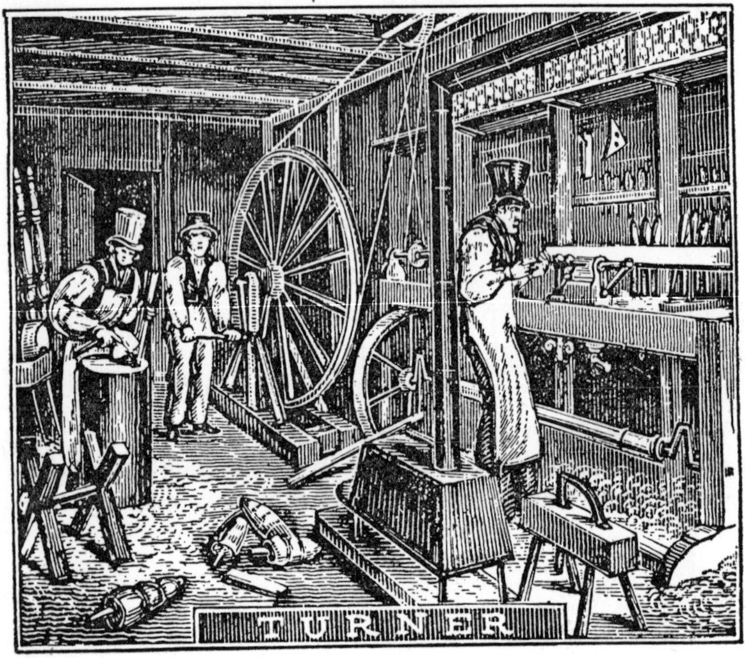
TURNER

5

Secret Hiding Places

IN many New England homes the grandfather clock in the hall was frequently used as a hiding place for money or small valuables. Doubtless some clocks are still put to this use. In all tall clocks there is unutilized space at the bottom of the case which is admirably suited to this purpose. By opening the clock door, one can reach down inside quite handily to deposit or remove whatever may be kept there. If the weights happen to interfere because they have run down into the lower part of the case, it is a simple matter to get them out of the way by winding them up or pulling them up to the top.

My grandmother used her tall clock on the stairs to keep a charming little chestlike japanned box, containing a miscellaneous collection of treasured belongings, in—several old-fashioned lockets, a number of brooches, a few rings, two or three bracelets, a handful of chains and strings of beads, and similar small trinkets and souvenirs. They were of little intrinsic value, but she cherished them for their associations. I think she kept them in the clock not so much because she was afraid someone might take them, but so she would always know where they were.

A curious accident, however, discouraged her from using the clock for a hiding place. One night the household was aroused by a terrific crash which, though promptly investigated, remained a mystery until morning. It was then discovered that one of the clock cords, which from age had become as weak as a tired old cobweb, had parted and the seventeen-pound iron weight had plunged to the bottom, ruining my grandmother's treasure box.

Old cupboards which have been sealed up and covered with wallpaper have frequently been lost sight of for generations and then only accidentally been brought to light when the walls were scraped for repapering. Objects have sometimes been discovered on the shelves which were overlooked when these places were closed. One such find presented a mystery. The hidden cupboard was found to be full of old china. The house had been in the same family for two centuries, but no one could tell who it was who had sealed off the cupboard, or why the china had been left in it.

Fireplaces which have been closed for years and presumed to be empty have been found to contain handsome pairs of andirons with matching shovels and tongs, brass or copper teakettles, iron trivets, and similar articles. But it is easy to see how this could happen. The fireplace was probably shut off in cold weather and a

Secret Hiding Places 73

stove, perhaps a Franklin with brass ornamentation, placed before it. The arrangement was looked upon as merely temporary. But the stove was suffered to remain, and in the course of time everybody forgot about the things left inside.

Many old New England houses have secret hiding places dating from the days when there were few, if any, banks where valuables could be deposited. Some of these concealed cubbyholes were so ingeniously built as to defy detection without the most careful search. There is reason to believe that in some cases they have been forgotten and the present occupants of the houses are unaware of their existence.

There was a cleverly concealed hiding place in the old Charles Noel Flagg house, which stood until a few years ago on Washington Street in Hartford, Connecticut. On the attic stairs, a few steps up from the bottom, was a landing, the tread of which was a sliding trap door that could be pulled out, giving access to the space under the stairs. There was room enough in this secret closet for a number of persons to hide, but it was used in the old days for the storage of valuables when the family was away. This old house predated any bank in Hartford.

The custom of paneling certain parts of the interiors of old houses gave an excellent opportunity for the construction of secret recesses. The pine panelwork around the fireplaces was often the best in the house, and it was also a favorite location for hidden nooks. In one eighteenth-century house I know there is a pair of small unconcealed cupboards over the fireplace, one at each end of the mantel. They look innocent enough, but both have false backs, which, if you take everything out of the front part, can be opened, disclosing behind each a spacious inner cupboard no one would dream existed.

Incidentally, in the early days of Lynn, Massachusetts, when haste and necessity prevented the construction of anything but the simplest habitations and people who had wealth were advised to abstain from all superfluous expense, no less a person than the Deputy Governor, Mr. Dudley, was censured for wainscoting his house.

No secret was made in former times of the fact that the Communion vessels of many Churches were kept in a closet under the pulpit. Since these vessels were frequently of wood or pewter, perhaps less care was taken for their safety than later for the silver Communion services, though people prized their pewter highly and often willed pieces to the Church.

Sometimes even the Church silver was stored in the meeting house. In 1805, when the church in Danvers, Massachusetts, was burned, the silver Communion vessels were lost, though the pewter ones were saved. In this instance the suspicion intruded that the silver was stolen rather than destroyed.

The deacons of the New England Churches had charge of the Communion vessels and the silver ones were usually kept by one of them in his home. Presence of mind on the part of the wife of a deacon saved the Communion silver of the Congregational Church of Fairfield, Connecticut, during the Revolution. The collection included two beautiful bell-topped tankards, two chalices, three beakers, and a cup with a handle, all still in the possession of the Church, I believe. These silver vessels were in the custody of General Silliman, one of the deacons of the Church, when on Saturday night, May 1, 1779, a British raiding party landed secretly near Fairfield and, proceeding to the general's house, carried him off a prisoner. Awakened by the noise of the soldiers breaking in, Mrs. Silliman hurriedly threw some bedclothes over the silver, which happened to be in a corner of the bedroom, where it was overlooked by the raiders when they ransacked the house.

In the *New Haven Journal and Courier* for July 15, 1853, the Reverend Leonard Bacon—his sister Delia launched the Baconian theory of the authorship of Shakespeare's plays and then went mad—told an interesting story concerning the silver baptismal basin belonging to the Center Congregational Church of New Haven. This large basin, the work of Kneeland, the Boston silversmith, was presented to the Church in 1735 by the will of Jeremiah Atwater, a wealthy local merchant.

Some years earlier Atwater had purchased a cargo of nails in Boston. Concealed in one of the kegs, under a layer of nails, he discovered a quantity of silver coins, amounting in value to the then considerable sum of fifty pounds. He wrote immediately to the Boston merchant from whom he had bought the nails, telling him of his find and inquiring as to the rightful owner, to whom he wished to restore the money. The Boston merchant replied that he did not know who the owner was, nor was it possible to trace him, as the keg had passed through many hands. He added that, since the keg was sold as nails and bought as nails, it was for Mr. Atwater to say what should be done with the money.

According to family tradition, Mr. Atwater, after thinking the matter over, decided to give the keg to the Church in the form of a silver baptismal basin, which he had made in Boston. The evidence, however, points to his simply having left the money to the Church and the basin having been made after his death in 1732. For in his will which was made that same year he provided as follows: "I give and bequeath unto the First Church of Christ in New Haven the sum of fifty pounds to be improved for plate or otherwise, as the pastor and deacons shall direct."

An interesting sequel to this tale of the cash hidden in the keg occurred many years later. When the British attacked New Haven, July 5, 1779, and entered the town, the baptismal basin and the rest of the Church silver was in the charge of Deacon Stephen Ball, who hid it in the chimney of his house at the corner of Chapel and High Streets, where it remained undiscovered by the invaders.

The vessels for the sacrament belonging to the South Congregational Church in Hartford, Connecticut, were put away for safekeeping and lost sight of and forgotten for many years. In 1839 a committee was appointed to procure six silver cups and three silver platters. The following year they reported that the new vessels had been purchased, agreeable to the pattern approved by the Church, for the sum of one hundred and ninety-one dollars, half of the money having been raised by subscription, the balance by selling old silver belonging to the Church. The new silver was inscribed *Second Church of Christ, Hartford, Ct., Jan. 1840,* and the inscriptions on the antique vessels sold were carefully copied. These showed the gift of a tankard by John Ellery in 1746, two cups engraved *The Dying Gift of Mr. Richard Lord to the Second Church of Christ in Hartford,* and two other pairs of cups marked only with the initials of the donors.

About 1861 certain Church officials unfeelingly converted more of the old silver into a bright and shiny silver-plated Communion service to replace the one purchased in 1840. Some twenty years after the plated service was acquired, the pastor of the church, Dr. Edwin Pond Parker, on looking over the old records, became interested in the fate of the vessels purchased in 1840. Had they been exchanged or were they still in existence?

"Talking one day with the late Deacon Charles Gillette, then president of the First National Bank," said Dr. Parker, "I was told by him that in the vault of the bank was an old and curious wooden box, which had been there for many years, but of the ownership or contents of which nothing was known by the officers of the bank. It was decided to overhaul and examine the box, and when the screws had been drawn and the lid removed, lo! snugly and securely packed therein were the cups and plates described in the report of 1840."

The Church now has nothing older than this 1840 silver, with the exception of a beautiful tankard given by William Stanley in 1787, which in some way escaped being thrown into the melting pot.

People in bygone days had the habit of converting

their savings into silverware. Silver in any form, whether minted into coins or hammered into spoons, teapots, candlesticks, porringers, or trays, had a certain definite value. Paper money was not worth a continental, and banks being either nonexistent or scarce, and there not being the confidence in such institutions that there is today, a person having Spanish dollars or other coinage was quite apt to take the money to the local silversmith to be made into useful articles, which, when the need arose, could be easily turned into cash or bartered at a more or less established rate of exchange. Meanwhile, some safe place to keep the silver had to be provided, particularly when no one was around to protect it, and hence the necessity for secret recesses.

For keeping money, papers, and small articles of value, desks, writing tables, cabinets, and other pieces of furniture were frequently fitted with secret drawers or compartments, which were so cleverly contrived that their existence has often been discovered only by accident. One day, a collector who had owned an old cabinet for years saw a piece of tape seemingly caught between two sections. When he pulled it a drawer came out which he had known nothing about.

A large antique walnut desk belonging to the writer has two secret drawers. The main feature of the interior is a small center cupboard flanked by pigeonholes and little drawers. On each side of the cupboard door is a fluted upright, like a diminutive pilaster, an inch and a half wide. These decorative pieces are the fronts of two narrow drawers which pull out, affording a place to keep papers. The small pilasters are so neatly fitted into

Secret Hiding Places

the desk and seem so inevitably a part of the design as to deceive anyone.

Inside what is called a well desk there is a rectangular recess several inches deep under the flat surface in front of the pigeonholes. Occupying a portion of the space usually taken up by the top drawer of the lower part, this well, which is a convenient place to keep stationery and correspondence, is revealed when a section of the flat surface is opened, as one would raise or remove the lid of a box. Although as a rule no secret was made of the existence of this compartment, I have seen a desk in which it was concealed.

Even writing boxes or table desks had secret hiding places for papers. One I recall had a false bottom. A section of one end slid out disclosing the private compartment. A cabinetmaker's apprentice, to show what he could do, often made a desk with ingenious secret contrivances of his own devising.

Chests, too, sometimes had secret sections. An important find of public documents was made in one that was being used as a grain bin in a Bay State barn. The father of the finder had been first selectman of the town and had kept the records in a hidden compartment at one end of the chest, but had died without disclosing their whereabouts. The discovery by the son defeated a lawsuit that was pending against the town for the recovery of money which the records showed had been paid.

The secret contents of many a piece of furniture has proved far more valuable than the piece itself. Finds have been made in the upholstery of chairs and sofas and the hollow legs of tables. Rare prints have been discovered in frames behind prints of no value, the real work of art having been concealed through ignorance.

Books have often been used to hide money. I knew a person who always kept fifteen or twenty dollars on hand in a copy of *Vanity Fair*. A famous instance of this kind is that of the man who died leaving a slip of paper with the message *$1000 in till*. Nobody knew of his ever having a cash register and it was not until after his collection of books had been sold that the executor recalled that among them was a folio edition of *Tillotson's Sermons*. Thinking this might be the *till* referred to on the piece of paper, the executor went to the bookseller who had bought the library, and finding the volume of sermons had not been sold, purchased the book. Dispersed between the leaves was the money. Oddly enough, the bookseller had sent the book out on approval, but the prospective customer did not like the binding, and had returned it.

Boxes made to resemble books have been used as receptacles for valuables. Real books have also been made into containers of this kind by hollowing out the insides. This is done by pasting the margins of the leaves together throughout the book and then cutting out the printed part of the pages. Colonel Samuel Colt, the Yankee arms manufacturer, once had a book box made resembling a Bible, with the title COLT'S BIBLE stamped on it in gold. Inside was one of his revolvers.

Book bottles, which were made to look like books but were actually metal containers, were a popular novelty in the last century and were in demand during prohibi-

Secret Hiding Places

tion. They usually had facetious titles such as *Our Mutual Friend, Paradise Regained, Ten Nights in a Barroom*, etc. Though properly classifiable as "books which are no books," bibliophiles have not scorned them.

Books have also been used to conceal doors. Sometimes this is done by covering a door with fake book backs, but a more effective way is to have the door a real bookcase filled with books. I recall a private library where a section of shelves in the book-lined room swung out to reveal a narrow stairway leading to the master bedroom above. Despite the weight of the books, the door opened easily. It was provided as a means of escape for the owner when someone came to call he did not wish to see. The house, which is still standing, is an old one, but the library with the secret door and stairway is in a wing added less than half a century ago.

In the parlor of the house occupied by the Fall River Historical Society a false bookcase formerly hid the entrance to a wine cellar where runaway slaves were concealed. This and other New England houses which were stations on the Underground Railroad to Canada before the Civil War usually had some sort of hiding place for fugitives, generally in the cellar, and occasionally with a subterranean passage leading outward.

Some New England houses had secret chambers. Perhaps the most famous was the hiding place in the minister's house at Hadley, Massachusetts, where the judges of Charles I were concealed for many years. Soon after the restoration of the monarchy many of the judges who condemned the king to death were apprehended and executed as traitors. Among those who made their escape were Goffe and Whalley, both generals in Cromwell's army. Shortly after they reached Boston in 1660, an order for their arrest came from Charles II, and the king's commissioners, eager to execute the order, compelled the judges to take refuge in woods, caves, and other places of concealment. Had the fugitives not been secretly aided by the colonists they would undoubtedly have been captured. For three and a half years they hid in New Haven and vicinity, sometimes in a cave, at other times in the cellars of the houses of their friends. Once while hiding under a bridge they heard their pursuers cross it on horseback.

In October, 1664, they set out for Hadley, traveling only at night, and at length arrived safely at the home of the Reverend John Russell, the minister of Hadley.

> The house of this friendly clergyman [reads an old account], situated on the east side of the main street, near the center of the village, was of two stories with a kitchen attached, and ingeniously fitted up for the reception of the judges. The east chamber was assigned for their residence, from which a door opened into a closet, back of the chimney, and a secret trap door communicated with an under closet, from which there was a private passage to the cellar, into which it was easy to descend in case of a search. Here, unknown to the people of Hadley, excepting a few confidants and the family of Mr. Russell, the judges remained fifteen or sixteen years.

The story of the sudden appearance of General Goffe when Hadley was attacked by the Indians during King

Secret Hiding Places

Philip's War is a well-known episode of New England history. The assault took place June 12, 1676.

When the people were in great consternation [says Hoyt, the historian of the Indian wars] and rallying to oppose the Indians, a man of venerable aspect, differing from the inhabitants in his apparel, appeared, and assuming command, arrayed them in the best manner for defence, evincing much knowledge of military tactics, and by his advice and example continued to animate the men throughout the attack. When the Indians drew off, the stranger disappeared, and nothing further was heard of him. Who the deliverer was, none could inform or conjecture, but by supposing, as was common at that day, that Hadley had been saved by its guardian angel. It will be recollected that at this time the two judges, Whalley and Goffe, were secreted in the village, at the house of the Rev. Mr. Russell. The supposed angel, then, was no other than Gen. Goffe, who, seeing the village in imminent danger, put all at risk, left his concealment, mixed with the inhabitants, and animated them to a vigorous defence. Whalley, being then superannuated, probably remained in his secluded chamber.

The Russell house with its secret arrangements was standing as late as 1794.

In the Thomas Thaxter house in Hingham, Massachusetts, built in 1652, there was a blind passage with a secret door, which Tories used as a hiding place from the Committee of Safety, pending their escape to Boston. The house was demolished in 1864.

There are numerous legends of buried pirate treasure

along the seacoast of New England and in many places at different times there has been a good deal of prospecting with pick and shovel for this hidden wealth. Some accidental recoveries have been made from the earth, but nothing of a value to suggest that it was the treasure of some old sea rover. No great hoards of gold and silver ingots, doubloons, moidores, and pieces of eight, Church candlesticks and chalices, or heaps of glittering jewels have been unearthed. There are plenty of stories of such discoveries, tales of men who have become suddenly and mysteriously rich, but in no verifiable instance has the finding amounted to more than a few hundred dollars and a few trinkets. It is true that small crockfuls of old coins, some dating back to pirate times, have been recovered, but it seems certain that these modest caches were those of early settlers.

Throughout New England wells were formerly favorite hiding places for personal property. Hanging small articles down a well was a quick and simple method of concealment, and it was easy to fish them out again. It is said that President Timothy Dwight of Yale College, who took his politics as seriously as he did his religion, was so fierce in his denunciation of the "infidel Whigs" that a New Haven woman, a parishioner of his Church, hung her Bible down the well for fear the infidels would get it.

Trees have also been used for hiding places. The town of Winterport on the Penobscot River in Maine had a famous tree called "The Bacon Tree," a giant pine amid whose branches the inhabitants hid their provisions and valuables when the British raided the river settle-

Secret Hiding Places

ments during the War of 1812. Flitches of bacon, hams, and sacks and baskets filled with the people's most precious personal possessions were suspended from the limbs of the ancient pine. Discovery of this communal hiding place would have given the raiders a rich haul, but they failed to notice the strange fruit hanging from the boughs of the Bacon Tree.

Hollow trees have likewise been used to secrete things. A notable instance was the hiding of the charter of the Colony of Connecticut in the historic oak tree in Hartford. When Sir Edmund Andros demanded the surrender of the charter, which the people had no intention of yielding, and was about to seize it as it lay on the table in the Council Chamber, the candles were suddenly put out and when light was restored the charter was missing. Captain Wadsworth had taken it and hidden it in the hollow trunk of the old oak tree. By this act the rights and privileges of the colony were preserved.

Among the antiques in the possession of the Historical Society of Nashua, New Hampshire, is a gun with an interesting history. On September 4, 1724, two Nashua men, Nathan Cross and Thomas Blanchard, crossed the Merrimack River to gather turpentine from pine trees. As it was a rainy day, they hid their guns in a hollow log to protect them from the weather. While busy in the woods they were surprised and captured by a band of Indians. Alarmed by the absence of the two men, the settlers organized a searching party to look for them. The rescuers picked up the Indian trail and followed it up the river. The Indians lay in wait for them and killed eight of the nine men in the party. Blanchard and Cross were led captive to Canada, where they were forced to remain several years, until at length they were able to purchase their freedom. When they returned to Nashua they looked for their guns and found them in the hollow log where they had hidden them years before. Cross's gun is the one now in the collection of the Nashua Historical Society.

MARINER

6

Antiques with a Pinch of Salt: The Seaport Towns and What to Look for There

ONE finds many antiques of a nautical character in the old seaport towns of New England. They are relics of the days of sail, when every other man you met in the street could properly be hailed as shipmate, skipper, or captain, and men spoke of the remotest places in the world as if they were neighboring towns.

The sea played an important part in the cultural development of these places. Almost every home had its cabinet or whatnot of treasures, its shelves laden with sandalwood and lacquer boxes, pieces of carved ivory and jade, shell and bead necklaces, queer bracelets, chopsticks, sets of chessmen, and many other odd things.

Lucy Larcom, writing of her girlhood in Beverly,

Massachusetts, during the second quarter of the last century, said:

> The women of well-to-do families had Canton crape for shawls and Smyrna silks and Turk satins, for Sabbath-day wear, which somebody had brought home for them. Mantel-pieces were adorned with nautilus and conch-shells, and with branches and fans of coral; and children had foreign curiosities and treasures of the sea for playthings.

The first collectors and the first museums were in the coastal towns. Salem was noted for its collections of natural and historical relics. The motto of the town was "The wealth of the Indies to the uttermost gulf" and many of the grand old houses were full of rare and valuable things. One of the best museums in the country, a storehouse of antiquarian and artistic interest, was established here during the latter part of the eighteenth century.

Nantucket likewise had its collections. The museum connected with the Nantucket Athenaeum contained a large number of curiosities, consisting chiefly of weapons, dresses, and utensils from the Pacific Islands.

Even the inns in seaport towns had collections. Herman Melville described an old hostelry near the water front in New Bedford when that place was a whaling center. The walls of the entry were hung all over with a heathenish array of monstrous clubs and spears and rusty old whaling lances and harpoons, some of them storied weapons. On one side of the public room, with its ponderous beams and wrinkled floor planks, stood a long, low, shelflike table covered with cracked glass

Antiques: Seaport Towns, What to Look For 91

cases, filled with dusty rarities from the ends of the earth.

Today in the antique shops of these old ports one gets interesting glimpses of the past. The imagination is stirred by the sight of such things as spyglasses, compasses, barometers, ships' wheels, navigation lamps and lanterns, seamen's chests, charts, ship models, bottled and otherwise, ships' bells, curious shells, name boards, carved sternpieces, occasional specimens of scrimshaw work, ship paintings and prints, weathervanes, and similar objects.

Some of these things you are also likely to find in old ship chandleries which have degenerated into marine junk shops, and the prices asked are apt to be less than in the antique shops. Dealers, of course, frequently visit these places, but in one harborside place on the coast of Maine, which was filled with secondhand anchors, lengths of chain, coils of cordage, blocks, and miscellaneous marine hardware, I was given my choice of half a dozen old pine sea chests at six dollars apiece, which was reasonable enough. No two were identical, but they were all plainly painted, save in a few instances, with the former owner's name or initials. Each was equipped with rope handles and had a small compartment at one end which served the sailor for a ditty box. The lids were loose and the locks were either broken or the key was missing, but these were minor defects easily repaired. Dealers sometimes buy old chests to fix up and decorate. One I saw had been painted a Chinese red, with ships and compass cards and other sea symbols in black and white.

In another marine junk store a man I know purchased

a tall binnacle, complete with compass and oil-burning copper side lamps. There was no telling from what ship it had come, but the compass bore the name of an English instrument maker. What does a landlubber do with a secondhand binnacle? The person who bought this one made effective use of it as a garden ornament, placing it in a spot where ordinarily you would expect to see a sundial or a bird bath. It became a strong point of attraction and interest.

Once, on a wharf, I bought the carved fashion piece of an old vessel. It was a graceful strip of scrollwork six or seven feet long, beautifully designed and carved in relief from a single plank. Traces of gilt still showed on the raised parts of the design. Exposure to the salt air had aged and dried out the wood until it was a silvery gray and seemed to weigh nothing at all. I placed it over the mantel in the seaside house where I was then living and few things have given me more pleasure.

It was undoubtedly the work of a carver of ship figureheads. A figurehead was, of course, the most outstanding part of a ship's decoration, but the sternpiece was also important, and some of the best work of the ship carvers was expended on the after end. The American eagle was a favorite motif. It was usually a fierce-looking bird, beaked and membered yellow, with outspread wings. It was generally shown supporting a shield or clutching a ribbon or olive branch which streamed gracefully across the stern. The color combination commonly used to set off the carving was gilt on black.

The most popular subject for a figurehead was the full-length female figure in flowing robes. Sometimes

Antiques: Seaport Towns, What to Look For 93

the person depicted was Columbia in a liberty cap, but more often it was a likeness of the person for whom the vessel was named, perhaps the wife or daughter of the owner.

Pioneers, Indians, statesmen, and merchants were also frequently represented. On small vessels it was the practice to use busts instead of full-length figures. But in any case the figurehead was almost always placed on a scrolled pedestal.

The ship carver had to serve an apprenticeship. He was as a rule a youth who had shown an aptitude for whittling. At first he merely roughed out the figure, which was then finished by the master carver. Pine was the wood generally used. Fortunately, the work of these ship carvers was not confined to the decoration of vessels and for this reason it is not unusual to find in old shipbuilding towns furniture, mirrors, hanging shelves, ship models, and architectural ornaments carved by these men. This is notably the case along the Maine Coast.

Nathaniel Hawthorne wrote as follows of Shem Drowne, the figurehead carver of colonial Boston, who was the first American known to have attempted this art:

> From his earliest boyhood he had exhibited a knack—for it would be too proud a word to call it genius; a knack, therefore—for the imitation of the human figure in whatever material came most readily to hand. The snows of New England winter had often supplied him with a species of marble as dazzlingly white, at least, as the Parian or the Carrara, and, if less durable,

yet sufficiently so to correspond with any claims to permanent existence possessed by the boy's frozen statues. Yet they won admiration from maturer judges than his schoolfellows and were, indeed, remarkably clever, though destitute of the native warmth that might have made the snow melt beneath his hand. As he advanced in life the young man adopted pine and oak as eligible materials for the display of his skill, which now began to bring him a return of solid silver, as well as the empty praise that had been apt reward enough for his productions of evanescent snow. He became noted for carving ornamental pump-heads and wooden urns for gate-posts and decorations more grotesque than fanciful for mantel-pieces. No apothecary would have deemed himself in the way of obtaining custom without setting up a gilded mortar, if not a head of Galen or Hippocrates, from the skillful hand of Drowne. But the great scope of his business lay in the manufacture of figure-heads for vessels. Whether it were the monarch himself or some famous British admiral or general or the governor of the province, or, perchance, the favorite daughter of the ship-owner, there the image stood above the prow decked out in gorgeous colors, magnificently gilded and staring the whole world out of countenance, as if from an innate consciousness of its own superiority. These specimens of native sculpture had crossed the sea in all directions and been not ignobly noticed among the crowded shipping of the Thames and wherever else the hardy mariners of New England had pushed their adventures.

Considering the great number of figureheads made in New England in the days of sail, very few have survived. Some were washed away during storms, or were

Antiques: Seaport Towns, What to Look For 95

lost with the ships to which they were attached, while others were removed and permitted to perish from neglect when the old ships were dismantled and converted into barges. The best of those which were saved are now in museums, though every now and then you come across a good specimen outside an antique shop, where, like the cigar-store Indian of old, it serves the useful purpose of attracting interest and trade.

The infinite patience of the old-time New England sailors, especially on the whaleships, is seen in the wonderful pieces of small carving in wood and bone which were done as a pastime during long voyages. Seamen the world over have for centuries indulged in this hobby, but none has ever equaled the "scrimshaw" work of the Yankee whalemen. Exhibitions of it may be seen in the nautical museums at New Bedford, Nantucket, and Salem. Specimens are also to be met with in seaboard antique shops.

> Throughout the Pacific [Herman Melville wrote] and also in Nantucket, and New Bedford, and Sag Harbor, you will come across lively sketches of whales and whaling-scenes, graven by the fishermen themselves on Sperm Whale-teeth, or ladies' busks wrought out of the Right Whale-bone, and other like skrimshander articles, as the whalemen call the numerous little ingenious contrivances they elaborately carve out of the rough material, in their hours of ocean leisure. Some of them have little boxes of dentistical-looking implements, specially intended for the skrimshandering business. But, in general, they toil with their jack-knives alone; and, with that almost omnipotent tool of the

sailor, they will turn you out anything you please, in the way of a mariner's fancy.

Among the most delightful scrimshaw pieces were the many objects made in miniature. One of these was a small urn-shaped container with a cap that screwed on tightly. They were fashioned as a rule from the tooth of a whale on a homemade lathe operated by foot power and youthful whalemen bound to sea used them to catch and preserve the tears of their sweethearts when they bade them good-by. These sentimental trinkets were often made by the old hands on a ship and given to the youngsters going on their first voyage.

Patience and skill went into the making of earrings, necklaces, bracelets, combs, and other articles of feminine adornment, while Grandma was perhaps remembered with a snuffbox. Nor were the children forgotten. For these there were numerous doll-size objects, particularly tiny cups and saucers.

It took an experienced hand at scrimshaw work to make a "jagging wheel." These small wheels, which were beautifully made and more often than not fitted with a whale's-tooth handle, were used to cut cookies or to crimp or press the edges of piecrust together. Looking at one today, it is difficult to believe that anything so carefully wrought was used as a kitchen utensil.

Even more intricate and difficult to make was the collapsible wheel for winding yarn called a "swift." The delicate whalebone spokes of the wheel worked like the ribs of an umbrella and could be opened or closed. Fastened to the edge of the table by an ivory clamp whittled from a whale's tooth, a swift required more skill

Antiques: Seaport Towns, What to Look For

and perseverance in its making than almost any other piece of scrimshaw work. Women prized swifts highly.

Although not technically scrimshaw work, because not executed as a rule by mariners, mention may be made here of the carved and decorated powder horns which were generally rural or backwoods productions. As much patient work was bestowed on these necessary and significant implements of war and sport as on any scrimshawed article, and they show perhaps an even greater variety of subject matter. Alice Morse Earle, who knew a collector of powder horns, a man who owned or had examined some three hundred specimens, says, "Maps, plans, legends, verses, portraits, landscapes, family history, crests, dates of births, marriages, and deaths, patriotic and religious sentiments, all may be found on powder horns."

The making of ship models was another handicraft which whiled away endless days at sea. The miniature model in a bottle has puzzled many people. How did the ship get inside? Some have concluded that the glass must have been blown around the model, but this is incorrect. The ship was actually inserted through the mouth of the bottle with the masts and spars neatly folded on top of the hull. Then by means of threads which had been attached to them the masts were raised and stepped in place. It was the work of days to make and bottle one of these tiny ships.

Many hours of work also went into the making of the larger unbottled models. The rigging alone took a lot of time. The first model I recall seeing was a large clipper ship in a saloon window. Ship models were almost as popular with saloon keepers as was the picture of Custer's Last Stand. In the earlier days, nautical signboards with painted ships often hung outside salt-water taverns. They were used, of course, to attract seafaring trade.

Years ago, in Norwich, Connecticut, I bought a fair-sized model of a whaler. Several generations of boys in the family from whom I acquired it had played with the old thing and it was a wreck. Some of the spars were broken and the rigging was in a tangle. But it had a hollow hull of excellent lines. Like many peaceful old ships, it had painted gun ports to give the impression that the vessel was armed. Some youngster had tried to make these sham ports realistic by cutting through them with a jacknife. It was a crude job left unfinished. I thought the damage could be easily repaired, the spars mended, and the ship rerigged, but I never got around to doing anything with it, and finally sold it for much less than it cost me.

The old shipbuilders worked from models, but these were half models of the hull only. It was easier for them to take the lines of a ship from a model than from a plan. By looking at a model they could size up a ship and tell what she would be like and how she would behave when built, whether fast or slow and whether she would throw a lot of water and be a wet ship or a dry one. These things were more difficult to determine from a plan. Many of the old half models have been identified by name by taking the scale measurements and then searching the local custom-house records for the registry of ships of the same dimensions. Lincoln Colcord

Antiques: Seaport Towns, What to Look For

did this with some of the models in the Penobscot Marine Museum at Searsport, Maine.

Pictures of ships hold a strong fascination for many people. The old-time sailor frequently tried his hand at painting them and sometimes achieved a fair measure of success in a primitive way. Correctness of detail is important in these pictures, and however lacking in painting technique the old salt may have been, he had the necessary technical knowledge to picture ships properly. But the best work was done by the professional marine painters, who had an eye for the beauty of a ship's line and knew how to capture it. Before 1830 they generally worked in water colors. Oil paintings of ships are seldom older than that date.

While there were a good many native artists who specialized in ship portraiture, Yankee skippers also liked to have pictures of their ships made in foreign ports, and some that turn up are alien productions. A good many were the work of Chinese artists, as is evident not only from the background of the oriental ports in which they were done, but also by the technique used. Chinese waves, for example, usually have conventionalized lacy edges. These Far Eastern artists haunted the water fronts, soliciting business from the Yankee sea captains when they came ashore.

One of several ship pictures which I have picked up at different times in different places shows a tall ship standing out of a harbor under full sail past a headland on which is a lighthouse. It may not be a portrait of any particular ship, but I have always felt that it was and hoped to identify her or the line to which she belonged by the house flag she is flying, a blue, white, and blue burgee, with a red ball on the central white stripe. But no list of house flags I have consulted has that special private ensign. It would add to the interest of the picture if I knew the ship, but even without a name it is a fine, spirited painting in a good old-fashioned frame.

A much older and more dramatic painting shows a pirate vessel attacking a merchantman. There is no mistaking the pirate craft, because she is of the traditional low and rakish type and is flying the black flag with skull and crossbones. It is a fanciful production, but the ships are correctly represented as the pirate vessel closes in to board. It is painted in oils on homespun. The waves are rather primitively done, but there is depth to the water, and the ships themselves show native genius.

The influence of the sea is seen in the seaboard weathervanes. Wooden ones were often whittled by sailors on shipboard, and the figurehead carvers made many. Shem Drowne, the eighteenth-century Boston ship sculptor, made the famous grasshopper vane for the Old State House in Boston and the quaint Indian with bow and arrow that adorned the colonial-government administration building. Both these old copper vanes are now museum pieces.

The strictly maritime weathervanes took the form of ships, whales, fishes, and sea birds, though the eagle was as popular a subject on land as it was on the sea. Seaside churches sometimes had a ship or whale vane. Metal vanes were usually the work of the village blacksmith. I saw a large painted wooden fish which for years had been the signboard of a fish market successfully con-

Antiques: Seaport Towns, What to Look For

verted into a weathervane by simply mounting it on an iron rod, but I do not know what kind of a fish it was supposed to be. Today the swordfish is the most popular of the piscatorial vanes. There is one on the post office in Provincetown.

On some old New England houses brass whales are hung by the tail for doorknockers. Dolphins are also sometimes similarly used.

The old banjo-style barometers in rosewood, mahogany, or walnut are never American, but generally English. A good example in working order, with a broken arch and inlay, is worth from a hundred to a hundred and twenty-five dollars.

The antique shops along the coast have been a happy hunting ground for those interested in old wooden duck decoys. An artist I knew used to buy all he could find and after painting them sold them in pairs for garden-pool ornaments. He soon found, however, that it was easier and cheaper to order new ones from Sears, Roebuck. He bought pintails, to which he sometimes added fantastic combs and tails. This made them topheavy, but by experimenting with them in a bathtub he learned how to weight them so they did not tip over in the water.

The American China trade was inaugurated as far as New England was concerned in 1787, when the *Grand Turk*, owned by Elias Hasket Derby, a Salem merchant, returned from a two-year voyage to the Orient. She was the first of a long succession of vessels which plied between New England ports and the East. Counting the *Grand Turk*, Salem alone had thirty-five ships engaged in the China trade, which brought back mixed cargoes of tea, coffee, spices, silks, embroidered shawls, nankeen, feathers, fans, chinaware, lacquer, gongs, and curiosities of all kinds. The net was spread wide, for the Yankee captains went by way of Cape Horn and returned by way of the Cape of Good Hope. Outward bound they called at the North Pacific fur ports and Hawaii. They visited Canton, the Philippines, the East Indies, and heading homeward stopped at Mauritius and various European ports of call. During the course of a voyage a vessel's cargo might be turned over a dozen times. It was an immensely profitable business in which many fortunes were made.

The Yankee shipmasters and crews brought home to their families a rich assortment of foreign things. Corner cupboards were filled with beautiful sets and pieces of china for which the women of New England had a natural feminine partiality.

Nor was the importation of tableware confined to that of far Cathay. Much was also brought from Europe.

The courting glass, a small mirror not more than twelve by fourteen inches in size and often smaller, which is found in old seaport towns, is believed to have originated in China and first to have reached New England late in the eighteenth century. Pieces of painted glass were set into the crested frame, which usually has a picture or design under glass at the top. These curious mirrors were usually placed in a shallow box, from which they could easily be removed, and were hung, box and all, on the wall.

Another outlandish glass also found in New England

Antiques: Seaport Towns, What to Look For 103

seaports is the Balboa or Bilbao mirror, which sailors from Marblehead are supposed to have brought from Spain in the late eighteenth and early nineteenth centuries. The frames were wood and marble, with a top double scroll and gilt ornaments.

Although Chinese lacquer was easily damaged by salt water, a good deal reached New England safely. Toleware in the form of candlesticks, tea caddies, and boxes from China still turn up in Salem, Newburyport, and Portsmouth. Like the lacquer which inspired it, this toleware is often painted a brilliant red ornamented in gold.

Objects of oriental pewter are also to be found in these places and elsewhere along the coast. Incense burners seem to have been especially popular. Old Chinese pewter was generally so heavily leaded as to be unfit for dining-room use.

The fabulous days of sail helped to build up the stock of New England heirlooms with numerous quaint and curious things.

CABINET MAKER

7

Yankee Whittlers

THERE is an old New England saying that if you call on a neighbor you need not say good night until he begins to whittle shavings for the morning fire. Although whittling may seem an idle pastime, it was a Yankee institution that produced much skill and many inventions.

Elias Ingraham, the clockmaker of Bristol, Connecticut, while on a voyage to South America to sell his clocks, whittled from a block of wood a design for a shelf clock that became enormously popular. This was the so-called "Sharp Gothic" pattern. Unfortunately, Ingraham neglected to patent the design, probably because he did not realize he had a best seller, and it was widely copied by his competitors in the clock trade. Another Connecticut inventor, Samuel Colt, also while on a sea voyage, whittled the first model of his "revolving pistol." In view of all the whittling done in New England, it is not surprising that the country's first factory for the manufacture of pocketknives should have been established in Connecticut in 1843.

According to Samuel G. Goodrich, who wrote many juvenile books under the name of Peter Parley, there were several reasons why whittling was indigenous among New Englanders. In the first place, the country was full of a great variety of woods, many of which were easily wrought and invited boyhood to try its hands upon them. In the next place, labor was dear, and children were led to supply themselves with toys or to furnish some of the simpler articles of household use.

> I can testify [he said] that, during my youthful days, I found the penknife a source of great amusement and even instruction. Many a long winter evening, may a dull, drizzly day, in spring and summer and autumn—sometimes at the kitchen fireside, sometimes in the attic, amid festoons of dried apples, peaches, and pumpkins; sometimes in a cosy nook of the barn; sometimes in the shelter of a neighboring stonewall, thatched over with wild grape-vines—have I spent in great ecstasy making candle-rods, or some other simple household goods, for my mother, or in perfecting toys for myself and my young friends, or perhaps in attempts at more ambitious achievements.

These occupations, Mr. Goodrich went on to point out, were instructive. The mind was stimulated to inquire into the mechanics of things, while the hand was educated to mechanical dexterity.

> Why is it [he asked] that we in the United States surpass all other nations in the excellence of our tools of all kinds? Why are our axes, knives, hoes, spades,

plows, the best in the world? Because—in part, at least—we learn, in early life, this alphabet of mechanics theoretical and practical—*whittling*. Nearly every head and hand is trained to it. We know and feel the difference between dull and sharp tools. At ten years old, we are all epicures in cutting instruments.

Whittling was not just a childish thing which one put away upon becoming a man. What one learned in boyhood was only the beginning and one went on, almost as a matter of course, toward perfection. The inventive head and the skillful, executing hand thus became a general characteristic. It was a pleasure to watch a Yankee perform the simple act of sharpening a pencil, since it was usually one of the first things he learned to do properly with a knife. As when carving meat at table, he did it quickly and expertly, without waste.

Among the things which New Englanders liked to whittle were butter molds. These were usually round stamps with a handle for imprinting a pat of butter. The design was cut intaglio into the face of the mold. The wood was generally maple or cherry, now and then pine. Often a bridegroom would carve one for his bride, perhaps with her favorite flower. Birds and animals, especially the eagle, were popular. Some old ones have the letter of the family name, like *J* for Jones. Sometimes there was a design to suggest the name. Sidney Stewart, the antique dealer of Needham, Massachusetts, who has a large collection of butter molds, possesses one with a hand that belonged to a Mr. Hand. There were also rectangular box molds holding a pound of butter with the design cut in the top piece. Print butter, as it was called to distinguish it from butter in a crock or firkin, always sold for more than bulk butter. One old-time Yankee had a special mold with the letters *D.P.*, which he used when his wife made butter that did not turn out very well. The initials, he said, stood for Damn Poor. A mold before being used was generally scalded and then dipped in cold water to prevent the butter from sticking to it. Eventually they were made by machinery, but it is the hand-carved ones which collectors generally seek.

Salt boxes, some with slanting lids, likewise engaged the attention of the Yankee whittlers, who liked to carve the top part around the nail hole where they were hung on the wall with a sunburst or shell design. Tall, narrow boxes with open tops in which to stand the long clay churchwarden pipes, with a drawer below for squills, were similarly carved.

It was only a step from making such things for the home by hand to turning them out wholesale by machinery in small woodworking shops. Rolling pins, meat mauls, lather boxes, butter paddles, faucets of all sizes, buckets, spice boxes, cheese boxes, and thousands of broom handles at a cent apiece were made. The cheese box is believed to have originated in Goshen, Connecticut. One shop in Maine used to make millions of toothpicks for the Chinese, who, though they could have bought them cheaper from the Japanese, preferred those made in America. All kinds of woodenware are still made in Maine, where is located the oldest and largest wooden toy factory in the world. And well back from the seaboard is a factory where thousands of pairs of different-size oars, mostly of ash, are turned out.

The New England cabinetmakers and chairmakers, who laid the foundations for their careers as youthful whittlers, had at hand a ready supply of a variety of woods with which to work, and they studied the nature and quality of these native growths with the greatest care and affection. Those most frequently used were pine, maple, poplar, cherry, black walnut, white oak, beech, and birch. Mahogany was easily obtainable from the West Indies, where the best kinds grow in Cuba and San Domingo. This Spanish mahogany, as it is sometimes termed, was used for furniture in this country before it was in England. It was first employed about the beginning of the eighteenth century.

New Englanders were not sentimental about oak, as were the English. Walnut, which began to displace oak in England at the time of the Commonwealth, and which brought about many changes in design during the Queen Anne period, was popular in New England, where the native black walnut was well suited to furniture making.

The colonial joiners and chairmakers were particularly partial to maple and exploited it as it never was exploited in England. From the knotty sections of the common maple and the sugar or rock maple comes the so-called "bird's-eye maple." What we call "curly maple" is derived from the sugar species of the tree. A lot of veneering was done with it. Maple furniture of all kinds was in great favor for a long time.

Cherry was also extremely popular, especially in the Connecticut Valley, where many pieces of furniture richly colored by time have been handed down for generations. Eliphalet Chapin (1741–1807) of East Windsor, Connecticut, and Aaron Chapin (1751–1838) of Hartford, worked in cherry with singularly successful results. Their highboys possessed original features, particularly in the design of the bonnet tops. Like maple, cherry can be highly polished, and in other ways is well adapted to cabinetwork.

Although hickory is a tough wood and was generally used for the slender spindles in the backs of Windsor chairs, it was not otherwise used to any extent in furniture making, owing to its sensitiveness to moisture and heat, which detracted from its lasting qualities. The English furniture trade was quite unfamiliar with this American wood.

The work of the cabinetmaker was similar to that of the carpenter, but greater nicety and exactness were required. His business was to make furnishings to go into the houses built by the carpenter. Tables, stands, bureaus, sideboards, desks, bookcases, sofas, and bedsteads were among the household furniture made in the cabinet shops. Sometimes the cabinetmaker was called in by the carpenter to carve some of the interior woodwork of a house. Samuel McIntire (1757–1811) of Salem is famous not only for his furniture, but also for his carving of mantels, cornices, and doors, and for his work on the exterior trim of houses. He even made urns for gateposts. His carving on furniture is considered the finest ever done in America.

While the cabinetmaker made certain kinds of chairs, particularly mahogany ones with upholstered seats, ordinary wooden chairs were made by the chairmakers, who did nothing else. In constructing chairs, the specialist in these articles undertook several at a time, from a dozen to two or three times that number, cutting up a quantity of wood for the seats and the different parts of the frames before he began assembling them. Sometimes he purchased the parts already turned from a turner.

In making a bureau, the old-time cabinetmaker used pine or poplar for the frames and drawers, facing the parts exposed to view with thin layers of mahogany. After marking out the several pieces for the frame and drawers, he cut them out and reduced them to the proper form and dimensions. He then fixed thin pieces of mahogany to the surfaces of the parts requiring it. In preparing the solid wood for the mahogany veneer, he cut small, contiguous grooves into the surface with a little plane having a cutting edge composed of small notches and teeth. Glue was spread over this prepared surface and also over that of the veneer, and the two pressed together with hand screws. Before the screws were applied, the surface of the veneer was covered with a heated board called a "caul." Overlaying a plain piece of wood with a thin veneer of other wood was not done then as it often is today to cut costs. Wood was cheap in the days of the hand craftsmen and veneering was solely a method of decorating a piece of furniture with beautifully grained woods in a way that could not have been done by using solid pieces alone. Old veneer which was sawn by hand was thicker than the paper-thin veneer produced today by mechanical means.

The pieces forming the frame of the bureau were assembled with mortise and tenon joints. The drawers were then put together, the four sides being dovetailed. The bottom was affixed to the sides and front by the construction known as "tongue-and-groove" and nailed at the back. Nails were also used to keep the bearers of the drawers in place. The back of the bureau was generally made of pine or poplar, while the ends of the piece were usually solid mahogany. The bureau was finished with four coats of varnish, each of which was rubbed down, and the process completed with an application of a coat of linseed oil. Plenty of "elbow grease" was required to produce a fine surface. And occasional applications of oil and wax are necessary to keep antique furniture in good condition.

There were cabinetmakers all over New England from the time of the Pilgrims onwards. One of the earliest furniture makers, if not actually the first, was Kenelm Winslow (1599–1672) of Plymouth, who came over in the *Mayflower*. No community seems to have been too small to support a cabinetmaker, and in the large, thriving coastal towns there were many. Salem and Newport had craftsmen of outstanding merit. Samuel McIntire of Salem has already been mentioned. Other Salem cabinetmakers were Nehemiah Adams (1769–1840), Daniel Clark (1768–1830), William Hook (1777–1867), and Elijah Sanderson (1751–1825). Sanderson's brother Jacob and Josiah Austin were in partnership with him. They made furniture not only for the leading families of Salem, but also for export to the Southern states and abroad. Sometimes other craftsmen mingled their wares with those of the Sandersons to make up a shipment, which the shipmaster to whom

Yankee Whittlers

it was entrusted was frequently able to dispose of to his own and the makers' advantage.

John Goddard (1724–1785) of Newport, Rhode Island, was a famous early New England cabinetmaker whose work ranks with that of the masters, William Savery of Philadelphia and Duncan Phyfe of New York. Goddard is generally credited with being the first maker of block-front furniture, though some experts believe that the honor should go to another Newport craftsman, Job Townsend (1700–1765). Goddard's cousin John Townsend (1733–1809) also made block-front furniture, but it is not known whether Goddard's son Thomas (1765–1858), who inherited and continued his father's business, made any or not.

Like the silversmiths and the pewterers, the cabinetmakers were often men of prominence in their communities. Stephen Badlam (1751–1815) of Dorchester, Massachusetts, was a brigadier general in the Revolution, and Benjamin Frothingham (1734–1809) of Charlestown was a friend of Washington and an artillery major in the Continental Army. Frothingham's father was a cabinetmaker, as was also his son. All were named Benjamin.

Throughout the colonial period the New England cabinetmakers led the country in the production of furniture, though during the latter half of the eighteenth century the craftsmen of Philadelphia produced pieces of the highest quality in design and workmanship. Naturally they followed English models. The early cabinetmakers were not trying to develop a distinctive type of American furniture. They held to the traditions they had brought with them. They followed the changes in English furniture design closely, in so far as those styles were suited to the new and altered conditions of life on this side of the Atlantic. They aimed at producing useful wares that would last a lifetime and that they wrought well we know from surviving examples of their work.

But in spite of the fact that they did not deliberately seek to express themselves in a peculiarly American way, they nevertheless modified, changed, and developed the old styles and the new to such an extent that presently they were producing pieces that were essentially American. The American Windsor chair, for example, differed from its English prototype. Lowboys, which were popular in this country, rarely appeared in England. The butterfly table, which is thought to have originated in Connecticut, was as American as the Yankee bean pot, which also had its nativity there.

Influenced as the colonial cabinetmakers were by English modes, they still managed to get a great deal of variety and individuality of expression into their work. Simplification was one of their ruling passions. The purity and restraint of their work fitted the temperament and thought of the people. Severe outlines and simple surfaces resulted in furniture of great dignity. That they correctly interpreted the needs and feeling of the time is evident from the way their productions sold in the face of foreign competition.

Most Yankees in those days were Jacks-of-all-trades. They were used to making things for themselves. They whittled handles for their tools, fashioned yokes for their oxen, and often turned their hands to making simple furniture because they did not have the money to hire a cabinetmaker to do the work. It was an age of handicrafts in which everyone was a handy man. Even cabinetmakers frequently pursued other callings outside their specialty. They had to in order to make a living. In the small towns, a joiner might be a farmer part of the year and turn to making furniture during the months unfavorable to husbandry. But even these part-time cabinetmakers were skilled workmen. Although their productions may be found only in the vicinity of the places where they lived, the greatest interest attaches to them. In supplying the local needs in the furniture line, these artisans who began as juvenile whittlers built up a tradition that is today viewed with keen appreciation.

TIN PLATE WORKER.

8

Tinware and Yankee Peddlers

MANY of the things which turn up in antique shops today were originally sold by the Yankee peddlers, who went everywhere. When Thoreau visited Cape Cod a century ago people took him for a peddler. One elderly native, who remained skeptical even after Thoreau explained that he had nothing to sell, remarked, "Well, it makes no odds what it is you carry, so long as you carry truth along with you."

Many peddlers specialized in tinware, others in clocks, a few in spinning wheels, and some in chairs, to say nothing of numerous other specialties, and the horde of miscellaneous men who sold all kinds of Yankee notions. The peddler was a master at pleasing all tastes, and there was scarcely any sort of easily portable merchandise he did not carry. Even the children were remembered. There were toy whips and jews'-harps for the boys, dolls and neat check aprons for the girls, and chapbooks with woodcut illustrations and an elevated moral tone for both. The trunk or pack peddler was in effect a walking five-and-ten-cent store.

That there were peddlers in New England in the youthful days of the colonies is shown by the early attempts that were made to suppress them. The chief complainants were the established merchants, who in their petitions to the various local lawmaking bodies pointed out that, while they paid taxes, the peddlers escaped that burden. In the interests of the public welfare, they also drew attention to the fact that the strolling salesmen were apt to be carriers of disease. But in spite of all the protests, the peddlers seem to have been left largely free to carry on their activities, probably because at that time there were not enough of them to constitute a peril, and people generally welcomed their visits, as they brought news of the world.

One day early in the eighteenth century a peddler appeared in the town of Franklin, Connecticut, once part of Norwich, with a stock of wares which for richness and luxury had never before been seen in that settlement. A farmer named Micah Rood, whose cupidity was excited by the dazzling display, asked the peddler to his house, where he stabbed him to death under an apple tree, the blood of his victim seeping down through the earth to the roots. The following spring the blossoms of the tree turned from white to red. This was disturbing enough, but when the fruit ripened in the fall, each of the large, yellow, juicy apples from the tree contained a drop of blood. Twice a year, in spring and autumn, Micah was reminded of his crime, which preyed on his conscience so heavily that he fell into dark brooding spells, neglected his work, and let his farm go to dereliction and decay. From a prosperous husbandman he sank to the status of a town pauper. The apple tree became the parent of many others, all with the same characteristics, and the so-called Mike Apple or Rood Apple or Blood Apple was famous for years throughout eastern Connecticut. Legend says that the conscience-stricken Micah finally hung himself from the tree beneath which he murdered the peddler, but the town records show that after a long illness the wretched man died a pauper's death and was given a pauper's burial, December 17, 1728.

It was the manufacture of tinware that gave peddling its greatest impetus. The industry had its rise in Connecticut about the year 1740, when Edward and William Pattison began making culinary vessels in the town of Berlin. The Pattison brothers, who were tinsmiths by trade, had come over from Ireland two or three years before, but they had been prevented from following their craft because they could not get the necessary sheets of tin. Eventually, however, they succeeded in securing a supply from England, and were soon turning out a variety of household utensils. They were the first makers of tinware in America.

Tinsmithing was then entirely a hand trade. The tinplates used were thin sheets of charcoal-smelted iron which had been reduced in a rolling mill and then coated with melted tin—three dips for what was called single tinplate, six for durable tinplate. Both kinds were heavier and more lasting than the light tin used today.

The tinsmith, in working the sheets up into various utensils, such as pans, pails, plates, teapots, coffeepots, bake ovens, measures, and cups, made patterns for the various parts of an article and having outlined these on a sheet of tin cut them out with a mammoth pair of shears. These were then brought to the desired form by a few simple tools specially adapted to the purpose. The various parts were then soldered together with a composition of tin and lead, a small charcoal furnace being used to heat the soldering iron. But before the tinsmith did any soldering he turned the edges of the parts which were to be united by beating them with a mallet on a steel-edged anvil called a "stock." This was done to strengthen the seams and give the solder a chance to take hold. Iron wire was used to re-enforce the edges and handles, which required more strength than the tin alone possessed. With the growth of the industry, machines invented by Seth Peck of Hartford County and driven by water power were used to turn the edges. These machines greatly expedited the manufacture of the ware and helped to reduce the price.

There was little tinware in the colonies when the Pattisons began making it. What there was of it was imported and expensive. Many people were not familiar with it at all, but though the new native product was something of a curiosity, it was well received. Housewives were attracted by its brilliant silvery appearance and delighted with its lightness. It was easier to handle than the heavy iron pots and kettles with which they had been obliged to wrestle.

At the outset, the Pattisons disposed of their tinware

in Berlin and the neighboring towns by carrying it in baskets and peddling it from house to house. The business grew slowly at first, but as soon as the metal showed its serviceability the demand for it spread, and the Pattisons traveled farther and farther afield to supply the expanding market. They taught others the trade and hired adventurous young men to peddle for them. They were kept busy meeting the popular demand.

With the exception of the period of the Revolution, Edward Pattison continued to make tinware in Berlin until his death in 1787. The war put a temporary stop to the business because it was impossible to get the raw material. Parliament had passed an act in 1749 prohibiting the establishment of rolling or planing mills in the colonies. This was done in a deliberate attempt to stifle possible American competition with the English manufacturers of metal wares. There was plenty of iron in this country, but no known supply of tin, which was first discovered in Goshen, Connecticut, in 1829, by Professor Hitchcock of Amherst. England, on the other hand, had the famous mines of Cornwall and Devonshire on which to draw. These mines had been in operation since before the days of the Roman occupation and continued to be worked until late in the nineteenth century, when the discovery of rich alluvial deposits of tin in Malaya and Peru caused them to become largely derelict.

Following the Revolution there was a boom in the American tinware trade. The year Edward Pattison died his son Shubael built a large new tinshop in Berlin. He took wagonloads of his tinware to Canada, where he exchanged it for furs. There is a local tradition that John Jacob Astor was his companion on some of these Canadian trips. However that may be, the furs which Shubael brought back to Berlin were made into muffs by girls, some of whom came from Newington and other near-by towns.

Meanwhile, other Berliners, who had seen the Pattisons prosper and had learned the business from them, began establishing their own shops. These Yankee tinsmiths did not subscribe wholly to Emerson's mousetrap theory. They believed in making a superior product, but like the Pattisons they did not wait for the public to beat a pathway to their door. They took their ware out and sold it directly to the people. For some time they carried their stock of pots and pans in baskets or sacks on their own backs or on the backs of horses. Later two-wheeled pushcarts were substituted, but as these were not suited to long journeys, they were superseded by one-horse wagons, which were in turn succeeded to some extent by large vehicles drawn by two and sometimes even by four horses. At first the tinware was peddled chiefly in New England and New York, but with the improvement of roads the peddlers extended their travels to the West and South.

Timothy Dwight, writing of the roving Yankee peddlers, said:

> Every inhabited part of the United States is visited by these men. I have seen them on the peninsula of Cape Cod, and in the neighborhood of Lake Erie; distant from each other more than six hundred miles. They make their way to Detroit, four hundred miles

farther; to Canada; to Kentucky; and, if I mistake not, to New Orleans and St. Louis.

The scattered population of those days was mainly agricultural. Travel was slow and in many areas country stores were few and far between and the peddler filled a definite need. As the people began to acquire new ideas and discover new wants, the peddler added other articles to his stock of tinware. A writer of a century ago says that calicoes were often packed in the same box with tin pans; cotton checks and ginghams were stowed away beneath tin cups and iron spoons; coffeepots were crammed with spools of thread, papers of pins, and cards of horn, pewter, and brass buttons, and cakes of shaving soap. Lengths of ribbon could be drawn from the pepper boxes and sausage stuffers. Tablecloths of cotton or brown linen drew the admiring eyes of the women away from the brightness of the new tin plates and knives and forks, all WARRANTED PURE STEEL. There were shining scissors to clip the purse strings of the women and new razors to touch the men in tender places. Silk handkerchiefs and neckcloths —things till then unknown—occupied the husbands, while their wives covetously turned over and examined colorful ribbons and fresh cotton hose. And, as already noted, the children were not forgotten.

From a small paper-covered juvenile book called the *Little Jack of All Trades*, which was published in New England during the second decade of the last century, and sold extensively by the Yankee peddlers at twenty-five cents a copy, comes the following paragraph about the work of the cabinetmaker, which is worth quoting as having some bearing on the subject of this book. It carries, of course, the usual moral that was then the hallmark of all juvenile literature.

> The ingenuity of an art which can convert planks of wood into chairs, tables, bookcases, chests of drawers, side-boards, and many other essential household articles, is certainly very great; and is now arrived at a much higher degree of excellence than it ever was. Whether veneered with the most precious woods, or inlaid with ivory, gold, ebony, and mother-of-pearl, painted, gilded, and varnished, no cost of labor is spared to render every article exquisitely beautiful; but in the decoration of our houses, as in that of our persons, we may be led too far, and in coveting splendor overlook utility.

A tin shop employing five men could keep twenty-five peddlers on the road supplied with pots and pans. The men who sold the ware were now seldom the ones who made it. While most of them were capable of mending a broken pan or a leaky coffeepot, they usually disclaimed the ability to fulfill the function of a tinker, as the repair of an old vessel might interfere with the sale of a new one.

The peddlers usually started out in the fall, their brightly painted wagons loaded inside and out with shiny wares. The Southern States proved such a fertile territory for them that tinsmiths from Berlin and the surrounding towns were sent South with quantities of tinplate to keep the army of peddlers in the field supplied with all the tinware they could sell during the winter. At the beginning of summer, the peddlers sold their horses and wagons and after an absence of from six to eight months returned home by water to New York and thence by boat to New Haven. The extent of the tinware trade is indicated by the fact that immediately after the War of 1812 no less than ten thousand boxes of tinplates were manufactured into household wares in Berlin alone in a single year.

The peddler had to be not only a good salesman but also a shrewd trader, as he often had to take payment in country produce or personal property which he had to dispose of later. If he did not know the value or the market for the things he took in exchange, he might find himself with a load of junk he could not get rid of to save himself. But generally he knew these things better than those with whom he traded, with the result that he made a profit not only on his original merchandise, but also on the things he took in exchange. Old copper kettles, pieces of pewter, brass, broken clocks, decrepit spinning wheels, all sorts of household things were taken by the peddler in gracious accommodation of his customers, especially in backwoods districts where there was little money in circulation. Richardson Wright says that the peddlers were the first dealers in early American "antiques."

The socially vigilant Timothy Dwight thought that peddling was a low calling and the peddlers themselves a set of rascals. No course of life, he said, tended more rapidly or more effectively to eradicate every moral feeling. "Many of the young men, employed in this business, part, at an early period with both modesty and principle," he declared. "Their sobriety is exchanged for cunning; their honesty for imposition; and their decent behavior for coarse impudence. Mere wanderers, accustomed to no order, control, or worship; and directed solely to the acquisition of petty gains; they soon fasten upon this object; and forget every other, of a superior nature."

One recalls the stories of Yankee peddlers selling wooden nutmegs, basswood hams, and white-oak cheeses. These yarns were, of course, exaggerated, though no one would have put it above most of them to resort to such trickery if they had found it worth while. Even the local merchants in those days were none too honest in matters of trade, many of them purposely keeping their shops in perpetual twilight, so a customer could not see the shoddy character of the goods he was buying. There was doubtless more than a grain of truth in the old story of the storekeeping New England deacon who called out to his clerk, "John, have you dampened the tobacco?" "Yes, sir." "Have you watered the rum?" "Yes, sir." "Have you sanded the sugar?" "Yes, sir." "Then come in to prayers."

The peddlers were often full of plots and plans for taking advantage of the people living in isolated places. There was one who used to make a special trip every spring to Martha's Vineyard and Nantucket to sell women's straw hats. He repeated his visits until he had built up a good business, and the women of the islands came to rely upon him to keep them informed as to the latest styles in feminine headgear. One season, when the hats were tiny, he told them that it was the fashion to wear two hats, one in front and the other over the bun in back, and instead of selling his hats singly that year, he disposed of them in pairs.

Despite all that was said against them, the peddlers were not altogether a bad lot. Many men who distinguished themselves later in life began their careers as itinerant vendors of Yankee goods. It will be recalled that Whittier's schoolmaster

> Could doff at ease the scholar's gown,
> To peddle wares from town to town.

Multitudes of young men took to peddling because there was not much else for them to do. Farming conditions were too poor in many sections of New England to give the increasing population a living. Just as necessity was the mother of Yankee inventions and manufactures, so was it the cause of the growth of peddling. The peddlers, who were often benighted on the road and had to crawl into haystacks or bivouac in the open under the stars, were indefatigable in getting the local products to market and selling them. The importance of peddling was that it showed New Englanders they could reach out beyond their own borders for trade. It accounts for the wide distribution today of many different kinds of New England antiques.

Yet it was not always smooth sailing for the peddler. Sometimes the demand was for one thing, sometimes another, and whether or not a sale was made depended on the ability of the salesman to flatter or cajole people into buying. One peddler, writing to his Connecticut employer in 1814, said, *I have traversed the country from Dan to Beersheba, besides going to Albany, and I have not sold buttons or spoons to any amount.* Nevertheless the trip probably proved a success, because the letter writer hastened to add, *Tin goes extremely well.*

The distinctive wagon of the peddler was developed very early in the days of the tinware trade. In shape it resembled the old New England town hearse, a flat-topped, boxlike affair, with rows of compartments along the sides, one above the other, which the peddler opened up to display his wares. There was a curving dashboard in front and a baggage rack behind. The driver sat exposed to the weather, though he often used a large umbrella which fitted into a socket to keep off the rain. Lashed to the baggage rack were bags stuffed with rags and feathers and other things which the peddler took in exchange; the top of the vehicle was also sometimes piled with these things. On either side near the rear or across the back were racks of brooms. Tin pails hung from hooks along the sides at the top of the wagon or were suspended underneath. They made a cheerful clatter as the peddler proceeded on his way.

There were peddlers by sea as well as by land. There were vessels called "old junkmen" which used to cruise along the coast, particularly the Maine Coast, selling tinware, calico, and notions, as did the tin peddlers with carts by land, taking in exchange old rags, iron, and other junk. Vessels were even built and fitted out especially for the marine peddling trade. They were like floating general stores with shelves loaded with goods. They visited the islands and small coastal villages at regular intervals.

Maine had its tinsmiths as well as Connecticut.

Stevens' Plains, now within the boundaries of Portland, was the center of the trade, which was established early in the nineteenth century by Zachariah Stevens. A score or two of men are said to have been employed here in the tinware industry, but some of these may have been peddlers.

Connecticut, however, remained the center of this metal industry. For the first four decades of the nineteenth century two thirds of the nation's supply of tinware came from this state. During most of this period the raw material continued to come from England. In addition, both before and after the Revolution British tinsmiths exported quantities of finished tinware to this country, and it must be owned that they were pretty clever about it, too. Like the Staffordshire potters who decorated their china especially for the American market, the English tinsmiths painted their "japanned" tinware, or toleware, in the style now called "Gaudy Dutch" expressly to attract purchasers over here.

This competition was met by our native tinsmiths' likewise lacquering their ware and also improving their methods of manufacture so they could sell their products cheaper. A delegation of British manufacturers visiting the United States about the middle of the last century reported: "The class of tools commonly used by tinmen are almost obsolete in New England States. In a well-furnished tinman's shop there are about twelve different kinds of machines employed."

Japanned tinware originated in the Far East and reached America by way of Europe. The ancient Chinese art of lacquering or varnishing wood probably suggested that tin should be treated in the same way. At any rate, not long after the appearance of lacquer in Europe, japanned tinware began to be imported from the Orient and was soon being made in France, Holland, and Spain. It was the French who gave the name "toleware" to trays, coffeepots, tea caddies, and other household articles of painted tin. England was especially successful with the new ware, owing to the discovery of a superior varnish that was particularly well suited to the process. It could withstand heat and presented a smooth, hard surface that was easy to decorate. Vast quantities were made at Pontypool, the center of the trade in Britain. It was chiefly this English toleware which found its way to America during the latter part of the eighteenth century.

It was painted with brightly colored flowers and other designs on a field of solid color. While black was the most popular background, other colors, such as Chinese red, yellow, green, blue, and white were used. Sometimes the background was painted in imitation of tortoise shell. Gold or bronze was frequently used for decorating, in the manner of oriental lacquer. Even the Chinese-pagoda motif was used on tea caddies or canisters and other pieces. The rich, mellow colors and quaint decorations of the early imported and domestic toleware are what make it so desirable today.

Some toleware was stenciled, but most of it seems to have been painted free-hand, with the same design repeated on piece after piece. Since it was not produced for the luxury market, but was made in quantity for popular sale, not much time could be spent in decorating it. It passed rapidly through the hands of the decorators, who, because they had to work fast in a kind of fine, careless rapture, achieved great facility and freedom in the execution of the designs. It is this unconstrained and easy technique which distinguishes the mass-produced article from the more timid, painstaking, and stilted work of the village tinsmith turning out an article to fill a special order. Yet the primitive designs used by the local artisan are often more interesting than those of his highly commercialized competitors.

Another form of decoration was pin-prick or punched work. This was a raised or embossed design made by tapping a blunt instrument with a hammer forcefully enough to dent the tin but not to pierce it. This kind of ornamentation was done before the various parts of a piece had been joined together. The design was marked out on the reverse of the side which was to display the decoration, the tinsmith working on the inner side to raise the bosses on the outer surface. Occasionally the tinsmith engraved a design directly on the outside, with a sharp instrument. But chased tinwork whether punched or engraved was never so popular as toleware.

Although many of the things made of tin were for kitchen or pantry use, numerous articles were also made to be used in other parts of the house, among them candlesticks and sconces. The former were often japanned, but the latter with their polished reflectors usually were not, as they threw back more light when unpainted. Many sconces were fancifully made. There were also candle boxes and tinder boxes and, later, matchboxes. Tin lamps were common before glass lamps put them on the shelf.

The commonest of all lighting devices made by the tinsmith was the lantern, which for many years was of the traditional Paul Revere type, a cylinder of tin with holes pierced in the sides and a peaked top with a ring handle. The perforations through which the single candle inside shed its beams were made in a variety of patterns according to the tinsmith's fancy.

Another New England perforated tin piece was the foot warmer, with a wooden frame and handle, which was used in the meeting house on the Sabbath and in the family sleigh on weekdays. Many of these portable stoves have survived.

Almost everything the Yankee peddler carried in his wagon, from buttons to books, is now sought by collectors of antiques.

WATCH MAKER

9

Timepieces

NEW ENGLAND is good clock country, although in the beginning clocks and watches were almost as scarce as in Samuel Butler's Utopia, where they were prohibited. Except for a simple noon mark on the window ledge or doorsill, or an occasional sundial, or more rarely an hourglass, the first comers were generally without any means of measuring time accurately.

Old American hourglasses are now extremely rare. The early specimens were crudely made compared with the Jacobean glasses which were brought from overseas. The spindles of the native glasses were usually whittled, whereas those of the imported instruments were neatly turned. The New England makers favored the use of pine and maple, while the English craftsmen showed their usual partiality for oak, particularly for the larger glasses. On the Continent, particularly in Italy, walnut was the popular wood. Some of the European glasses which found their way to this country were decorated with inlay work.

Metal frames came later. Iron, copper, brass, and occasionally silver were used. The brass and silver hourglasses were generally engraved, often with mottoes about the fleeting quality of time similar to those seen on sundials. At times the frames were made of metal and wood. Since the pear-shaped glass bulbs were fragile and liable to break, the metal frames were sometimes made to slip apart so that new bulbs could be inserted, or the sand in the containers reached if the glass needed regulating by changing the proportion of the contents.

The flasks of the older glasses were not blown in one piece, but separately, and a leather or metal collar was placed around the necks, where they met, to keep them in line. Persons seeing old glasses of this kind have sometimes erroneously taken this for a defect, thinking the connection between the upper and the lower glass had been accidentally severed and a collar or band used to repair the break. A late order of hourglasses was made entirely of glass, with the bulbs united at their apices.

Foreign hourglasses of carved ivory are of rare occurrence in New England. They are generally small, sometimes made in pairs, and often beautifully wrought, and one wonders how objects of such delicate workmanship could have survived through the years intact. Their very scarcity shows, perhaps, that many became casualties.

Hourglasses may range anywhere from two inches to two feet or more in height, but size is not necessarily an indication of the length of time a glass was originally designed to measure, as this depended on the quantity and quality of the sand used, whether fine or coarse, and the size of the passage through which it passed from the upper to the nether glass. An old device was a rack containing a row of four hourglasses of identical size but running at different speeds, the sand in the first glass passing completely through in fifteen minutes, the second in thirty minutes, the third in forty-five minutes, and the fourth in an hour. By looking at this quartet of glasses one could tell approximately how many minutes of the hour had glided away. But it is impossible to say precisely what period most old glasses were intended to mark, as the grains of sand through friction have become finer and the aperture worn. In some cases mercury was used, but most of these old timekeepers were sand glasses filled with red, white, black, or purple particles.

The largest and smallest hourglasses were the nautical ones. The biggest ran for two hours and were used to divide the time on shipboard into watches, the glass running for four hours with only one turning halfway through the watch. The nautical expression "warming the bell" is a survival of the days when a sailor, in order to shorten his watch, made the sand run faster by warming the glass with his hands. Today a sailor who prepares to quit work well in advance of the expiration of his watch is said to "warm the bell." The small fourteen and twenty-eight second glasses, which were used when the lead was heaved to determine the vessel's speed, were called "log glasses."

Most hourglasses were made, as were the marine glasses, for certain specific uses rather than for marking time generally. One New England housewife who had a quaint antique three-minute glass inherited from her grandmother used it for years to time the family breakfast eggs. One night she handed it to a new maid with instructions to cook the eggs with it in the morning. The maid, who had never seen an hourglass before and did not know what it was, put it in the boiling water with the eggs and broke the heirloom. It was a double tragedy because the housewife also used the glass to time her long-distance telephone conversations with her daughter, to whom she would talk till the last grain ran out.

The sermon glass, which was almost as important an adjunct of the early colonial meetinghouse as the Bible, ran for twenty minutes, but the sermon did not end when the sand expired in the glass. Long sermons were then the fashion and a minister was to some extent judged by the number of times he turned the glass while preaching. One divine is reported to have said, as he reversed the timepiece on his desk, "Brethren, let's have another glass."

Many of the pulpit glasses were elaborately made. When the new meetinghouse was built in Hartford in 1739, Seth Youngs, a local clockmaker, was commissioned to make the sermon glass and also the gilded brass weathercock and ball for the steeple. His charge for the hourglass was six pounds, a sum which was thought to be exorbitant. The society remonstrated with him and the bill was settled for five pounds ten shillings.

Nearly a century before this, in 1640, a clock was left to the Hartford Church by the will of Henry Packs. It was an English brass lantern clock which was probably used by the drum beater or bell ringer to tell when it was time to summon the people to worship. In 1649 a similar clock was listed in the inventory of the estate of the Reverend Thomas Hooker, the first minister of the Church, but his successor to the pastorate, the Reverend Thomas Stone, had nothing but an hourglass when he died in 1663.

Sundials have been in use in New England ever since the first days, both the small pocket kind and the garden size. Roger Williams, the founder of Rhode Island, who came over in 1631, had a portable dial and compass, which he carried in lieu of a watch. Judge Sewall, another seventeenth-century New Englander, had a clock and a dial. These dials were doubtless of English origin. The inventory of the estate of the first Thomas Danforth, the noted pewterer of Norwich, Connecticut, who died in 1783, lists a dial mold. While pewter clock dials are not absolutely unknown, they rarely occur, and it is more than likely that the Danforth mold was designed for casting full-size sundials, though as far as I know none has come to light.

But with only hourglasses and sundials, how did people tell time in the middle of the night? If a person wished to be up and about his business before dawn, how did he know whether it was time to rise or not? The answer is that he looked at the stars. He had his almanac and he knew from the position of the constellations how far the night was gone. Even without an almanac, he was a pretty good judge of time, as he was habitually an attentive observer of the heavens.

Although New England, as already stated, is good clock-hunting territory, this is not to say that the searcher after extreme rarities will not do just as well in Pennsylvania, or nowadays perhaps among the dealers in the Middle West; but the vast numerical preponderance of all American clocks made before the Civil War was manufactured in New England, mostly in Connecticut, and the chances of picking up an attractive clock by a Yankee maker at a sensible price are much better than the chances of landing a seventeenth-century brass bracket clock or a grandfather by David Rittenhouse.

Scarcity raises the price of an antique. Fabulous rarity, on the other hand, simply discourages everyday collectors, who, though they may take un-Christian satisfaction in owning some piece that nobody else can have, are much likelier to take common ordinary satisfaction in a piece that they can have. And that means New England clocks.

An engaging feature of Yankee timepieces, furthermore, is that though there are thousands in existence, and perhaps hundreds available at any given moment, and though a lot of them are thirty-hour shelf clocks of the kind introduced by Eli Terry, even an inveterate clock fancier may go for years without ever seeing two exactly alike. This is easily explained.

In the first place, the competing manufacturers were innumerable. Nobody has fully straightened out even so limited a field as the Connecticut makers of woodenwheel clocks from 1816 to 1836. There were at least twenty firms or partnerships, for instance, which included members of the Terry family alone. Different labels immediately distinguish most clocks.

Second, though the movements or works are all much alike, even when made in different factories, the man who made the movement probably hired someone else to make the case. Around Plymouth and Bristol, Connecticut, movements passed current as money in trade for cases, or even real estate. And the cases, in turn, while probably either "pillar-and-scroll" or ogee in general style, varied endlessly with the whim of the case maker.

Supposing for the moment that you find two clocks by the same maker with identical movements and identical cases, which is most unlikely, you can still cover a small bet that the dial and the "tablet"—the glass panel below it—will be decorated quite differently. And if they aren't, you may offer a second small bet that some modern merchant has been cutting his losses by replacing broken glass.

Up to about 1790 all the Yankee clocks the ordinary collector stands any chance of owning were grandfather clocks, with weight-driven eight-day movements in tall wooden cases, nearly always with engraved brass dials. The movement might have lentil-shaped wooden wheels —these came from the Cheneys in East Hartford, Connecticut, and ran thirty hours at a winding—but much more likely the wheels would be of cast brass.

These clocks were never just alike. Each one was turned out as a separate undertaking by a clockmaker and his apprentices, if any. In the earlier parts of the eighteenth century he had to make his own tools and cast his own wheels, in which he then cut the cogs or teeth with a "clockmaker's engine." Even the engine was made by the clockmaker himself. It seems to have been the job of every apprentice toward the end of his time to make one of these machines for himself.

The old-time Yankee clockmakers were versatile mechanics, many of them combining other trades with that of clockmaking. Some were goldsmiths, silversmiths, tinsmiths, blacksmiths, pewterers, bell founders, jewelers, joiners, and Jacks-of-all-trades. Others were instrument makers, specializing in surveyors' and mariners' compasses. They also made such articles as swords, buckles, brass trumpets, cannons, copper stills, weathervanes, walking sticks, and spurs. Some practiced dentistry. Ezra Dodge of New London, who died in the yellow-fever epidemic which ravaged that town in 1798, was described as "a watchmaker, clockmaker, gold and silversmith, brass founder, gunsmith, locksmith, and grocer." He was an apprentice of Thomas Harland, the famous clockmaker of Norwich, Connecticut, who came over in one of the Nantucket vessels that brought the tea that was dumped into Boston Harbor. In 1787, Harland built a fire engine for the town of Norwich. A few years later his shop burned down, with the loss of all his tools and material.

According to Penrose R. Hoopes, the leading authority on the eighteenth-century Connecticut clockmakers, "Harland was one of the most important single figures in the history of early Connecticut clockmaking. He was well educated and a very skillful mechanic, his clocks were superior in workmanship and were made in larger numbers than those of any of his contemporaries, but his greatest influence was in the number of appren-

Timepieces

tices trained in his shop." By 1790 he is believed to have employed as many as a dozen apprentices, who assisted him in turning out forty clocks and two hundred watches a year. In the obituary notices printed at the time of his death in 1807, Harland was said to have made the first watch manufactured in America.

In 1797 a curious collection of clocks was exhibited at the Columbian Museum in Boston. The proprietor of the museum announced in the *Boston Chronicle* on December 19th that he had purchased a collection of concert clocks as a valuable and pleasing addition to his very extensive repository of curiosities. The collection included the following:

1. A Canary Bird, which sings a variety of beautiful songs, minuets, &c. natural as life.
2. A company of Automaton Figures, which dance to the Music of an Harpsichord.
3. Three Figures, which play the Organ and Clarinet in concert.
4. Three Figures, which play the Harpsichord and Hautboys, in concert.
5. King Herod beheading John the Baptist, and his Daughter holding a charger to receive the head.
6. A Chimney Sweep and his Boy on top of a chimney.
7. Three Figures which strike the hours and quarters.
8. A Butcher killing an Ox.

These clocks undoubtedly came from abroad, quite possibly from England. But musical clocks were also made by the New England clockmakers. Benjamin Willard, Jr., who was doing business in Roxbury in 1774, advertised for sale in the *Massachusetts Spy*, "A number of Musical Clocks which play a different Tune every Day in the Week, on Sunday a Psalm Tune." A year earlier Thomas Harland advertised himself as a musical-clock maker in Norwich, and there is still in existence a musical clock made by his former apprentice, Daniel Burnap of East Windsor, Connecticut.

Around 1790 a change took place in the clock trade. By that time the Doolittle Foundry in Hartford was selling most of the brass wheels and New England clockmaking had become a matter largely of buying, finishing, and assembling parts. But the dial had still to be put on; and nearly always the movement was sold by itself, without a case. The buyer might hang it up bare, as a wag-on-the-wall, for months or years before he could afford to have a joiner or cabinetmaker build a case. So there is no particular need to feel cheated if the movement and tall case which you buy didn't originally go together. These dials, incidentally, were usually imported, and often the cast-iron "dial plate" bore an English foundry mark; but that doesn't mean a clock isn't a real New England piece. A few years later somebody thought of pasting a paper dial on a wooden panel. If you find one of these over a wooden movement, and having pasted on *that* a paper disk signed E. TERRY, you will know you have one of the first batch of mass-produced clocks in the world. More about that in a moment.

Grandfather clocks went on being made through the first third of the nineteenth century. One very prolific maker then was Riley Whiting of Winchester, Connecticut. But by then two other varieties had sprung up to catch the eye of later collectors.

First in time, scarcity, and price (then as now) came the "banjo clock" of the Willard family. Simon Willard of Roxbury, Massachusetts, patented in 1802 a kind of wall clock that was usually cased by the maker himself in a banjo-shaped housing, the part for the movement nearly always round; the neck flaring toward the bottom, because the pendulum needed room to swing; and the bottom either round or rectangular. Occasionally the neck would carry a lyre-shaped front. Since these were "timepieces," with no striking mechanism, they ran by one weight, which hung down behind the pendulum.

Banjo clocks were expensive when first made, partly, no doubt, because they were never sold uncased. Today they command so much money in the antique trade that all kinds of monkeyshines are profitable. Among the easiest is adding a maker's name. Many banjo clocks were not signed, perhaps, as Carl Dreppard has suggested in his book on American clocks, because they infringed on Simon Willard's patent; what more tempting, then, than to double their value by merely lettering S. Willard, Patent on the panel?

After thus warning you that the name may be a fake, I will only remark that there were thirteen Willards in the clock business, nearly all in eastern and central Massachusetts; that Benjamin was the father of the tribe, having learned clockmaking from the first of the Cheneys, of Connecticut wooden-grandfather-movement fame; that Aaron and Simon made the banjo clock famous; and that Aaron's apprentice John Sawin (later Sawin & Dyar) and Lemuel Curtis produced banjo clocks as good as the Willards' own. Banjo clocks had cast brass movements.

Now we come to the clocks that the ordinary collector can afford, or at least find.

The old Cheney grandfather clocks, made in East Hartford, with hand-carved wooden wheels, had brass dials, ran only thirty hours instead of eight days, and are scarcer than blackberries in winter. But the Cheneys may have given lessons in wooden clockmaking to a young neighbor from East Windsor. At all events, the young neighbor, already a practiced maker of brass movements, must have known the Cheneys and their product. His name, Eli Terry, is the greatest in the world's clock industry—as separate from the clockmaking craft. He first applied the new Connecticut principle of mass interchangeable manufacture to clockmaking.

Terry's career spanned all stages of Yankee clockmaking. Born in East Windsor, Connecticut, in 1772, he was apprenticed to a local clockmaker, Daniel Burnap, who taught him how to make his own tools and clock movements. Domestic clocks at that time were all of the tall grandfather variety, the best ones with cast brass movements, the cheaper ones with wooden works. Both kinds were equipped with brass dials, which young Terry learned to engrave with ornamental patterns.

When Terry finished serving his seven years' apprenticeship in 1792, he went into business for himself in

East Windsor, making clocks to order, with either brass or wooden movements, depending on which his customers could afford, and these he fitted with silvered brass dials which he obtained from his old master, Daniel Burnap. Probably he did not get many orders for clocks, because a year or two later he moved to a community near Waterbury which in 1795 was incorporated as the town of Plymouth, Connecticut. That same year young Terry married, and the state of his affairs is shown by the fact that he and his wife are said to have gone housekeeping with only two chairs and two cups and saucers.

Terry at this period peddled his own tall clocks, or rather the works for them. Mounted on horseback, he could carry the movements of four grandfather clocks, one before, one behind, and one on either side of the saddle. As there were other makers on the road selling their clocks, Terry sometimes had to travel far afield to dispose of his own. He asked twenty-five dollars apiece for them, but was frequently obliged to take payment in country commodities, and often returned home loaded with salt pork. Sometimes he took the purchaser's note or sold his clocks on the installment plan. Collections were slow and difficult, but that was the way country clockmakers were obliged to do business.

One Yankee clockmaker, Gideon Roberts of Bristol, Connecticut, built up quite a trade peddling clocks in Pennsylvania and later in the South. While pedd^{li} Pennsylvania he became interested in the Qu^a of life, joined the Society of Friends, and a^d mode of speech and dress. Simon Willar^r

famous New England clockmaker who liked to peddle his own wares, particularly after his wife's death. Wandering about the countryside seemed to ease his sorrow.

By about 1800, handmade wooden movements were seriously crowding the more expensive brass movements. By 1802, when Simon Williard patented his banjo clock, Terry had the idea of producing wooden movements "for the wholesale trade" by water power, a dozen or two at a time. People in Plymouth, Connecticut, to which he had moved from East Windsor, thought this a "rash adventure."

In 1807 he made a contract with two brothers in Waterbury to produce four thousand wooden grandfather movements in three years, at four dollars per movement. The brothers had to supply the wood. The native woods used were oak, apple, laurel, and cherry. The wheels were of cherry. These are the clocks with paper dials that have the appliquéd T. TERRY label. If people thought twenty-five at a time rash, they couldn't decide whether Terry or the Waterbury brothers were the more dangerous lunatics to plan in thousands. Nevertheless the four thousand were produced on schedule and apparently paid for, which was worth remark in the clock trade of those days. It is not impossible that Terry's pay was at least partly a sixty-acre farm in Waterbury.

To a collector, these clocks have chiefly association and scarcity value; they are not handsome, or good timekeepers. As a matter of fact, all wooden movements tend to split off a cog here and there and in wet weather they swell up and stop. Wood was deliberately chosen as a cheap substitute for brass, and the buyer took this as part of the bargain.

Terry, a very conscientious workman, evidently thought no better of his first four thousand clocks than I do. He spent the years 1812 and 1813 experimenting on a complete novelty to the clock trade—a wooden-movement shelf clock, to be sold complete with case. Grandfather clocks had eight-day movements, but the short shelf case, a little over two feet high, did not allow the weights to fall far enough for this. Terry ran the lines over pulleys at the top of the case, thus gaining fall enough for a thirty-hour movement.

He fooled around with experimental models that did not satisfy him, one a simple wooden box with a curved top shaped like the dial of a grandfather; another having a plain glass front with the dial figures painted on; a third having the brass escapement wheel in front of the dial, and the pendulum hanging from it, likewise visible until it disappeared behind the painted tablet. These attempts, dating from around 1814 or 1815, are way out of our class; I have seen examples, so I know they exist, and that's all.

Then came the deluge. Terry and the other clockmakers around Plymouth took the wooden thirty-hour shelf movement as Terry perfected it (his patent was finally dated June 12, 1816) and cased it in an Empire box with pillars at the front corners and a bonnet or "scroll" on top. That was the TERRY PILLAR-AND-SCROLL CLOCK, a convenient, meaningless label perhaps devised by an auction cataloguer.

Much ink and temper has been wasted arguing over

who "invented" the pillar-and-scroll case. (Who invented the Empire bureau?) In all probability, Eli Terry neither knew nor cared; the "Terry's Patent" movement was what interested him. He licensed his former employee Seth Thomas to make shelf clocks under Terry's Patent, and Eli and his brother Samuel Terry supplied movements for thousands of clocks cased by other manufacturers, in addition to those issued with the labels of Eli Terry, Eli Terry & Sons, and Eli & Samuel Terry. Eli Terry, Jr., who died before his father, was also in business, first as one of the Sons, then for himself.

Along with the thirty-hour shelf clock came the custom of pasting on the inside back of the case a large label, called the "paper," which usually gave the maker's name, the promise WARRANTED IF WELL USED, and directions for winding and oiling.

To be really desirable as an antique, a shelf clock must have its original paper, pendulum, and weights. I know of one collector who got a New England clock with a particularly interesting paper for under thirty dollars, and has been congratulating himself ever since on buying the paper so cheap; he figures the clock was just thrown in. The dealer, on the other hand, knew he was selling a fairly late clock in nice condition at a reasonable price; he threw in the paper.

Differences of standpoint like this are what make Yankee antiquing inexhaustible fun. Connecticut shelf clocks, furthermore, offer a particularly wide field for such differences. If you must have an unmistakable Eli Terry Senior clock in prime condition, you will spend some time and a fair amount of money getting it. But if

Timepieces 151

you can be satisfied with a good clock of the type, there are no rules and few difficulties. You just spot a clock you like, make sure it's whole, and there you are. Whether the paper says SETH THOMAS, PLYMOUTH, or PRATT & FROST, READING, MASS., or SEYMOUR HALL & CO., UNIONVILLE, CONN., does not affect the look of the clock on your mantel.

The next step in Connecticut clockmaking was the return of brass movements. Cast brass wheels had to be shaped and filed down individually. Rolled sheet brass was substantially an English monopoly until 1823; up until then, a clockmaker trying to build a movement out of sheet brass had to cut up old kettles. But soon the brass supply outran the needs of the button industry, which had called it forth; and in 1832 Joseph Ives, a clockmaking genius at Bristol, Connecticut (the next town to Plymouth, where Terry, Thomas, Silas Hoadley, and Chauncey Jerome all got their start) patented an eight-day movement of sheet brass.

In 1838 a volatile young man named Chauncey Jerome, who had started in as a casemaker for Eli Terry, Sr., made the first sheet-brass thirty-hour movements in mass production. He later tangled with P. T. Barnum, bankrupting both parties, and in his old age he wrote a little book that all collectors of Yankee clocks should have: *History of the American Clock Business for the Past Sixty Years, and Life of Chauncey Jerome* (New Haven, 1860).

Eli Terry flooded the United States with clocks; Jerome and his competitors flooded the world. By 1840 Bristol alone was producing over thirty thousand clocks a year, at an average of eight dollars apiece, and Connecticut was producing a million dollars' worth. England and other foreign countries imported them at a tremendous rate.

An amusing situation developed when Jerome made his first shipment of clocks to England. The British customs officials could not believe that the value of the clocks stated in the invoice was correct. Nobody over there had ever heard of clocks that cheap. They thought the Yankee clockmaker was trying to evade payment of duty by fraudulently undervaluing his merchandise. Accordingly, they seized the clocks and exercised the government's right under the law of paying for them at the declared value plus ten per cent. Jerome was delighted. He had without expense sold all the clocks in one lot at a profit for cash. Another large shipment was dispatched and again the clocks were bought by the British government. By the time the third cargo arrived it dawned on the officials that Jerome's valuation was honest and the shipment was accepted in the normal way. The sale of the seized clocks by the British treasury had advertised Jerome's trade-mark, so that he found it easy to dispose of later shipments made in the ordinary course of trade.

This, naturally, is almost the end of the timepiece trail so far as New England antiques go. Some of the brass movements went into pillar-and-scroll cases, more into ogee mahogany veneer cases; there were fanciful designs like the acorn silhouette from the Forestville Manufacturing Company; but anyway the brass clocks grew so plentiful that there is not much triumph in finding them. Seth Thomas still makes some models strongly reminiscent of the Jerome era.

The Yankee clock collector should know, however, that the brass industry contributed another big change when Silas Burnham Terry discovered how to temper steel springs. Joseph Ives had already made a number of rather homely clocks driven not by weights but by an elliptical steel "wagon spring," and several contemporaries took out licenses under his patents. But the Connecticut-made steel coil spring, introduced about 1862, revolutionized cheap clockmaking and the whole industry of central Connecticut to boot.

From then on the chief interest in New England clocks centers on the preposterous cases the manufacturers contrived. For many years the old inn at Windham, Connecticut, told time by a cast-iron Connecticut clock in the shape of a Negro dancing girl with the dial over her stomach, who rolled her eyes as the pendulum swung. "Minstrel Sambo" and a Continental soldier were also equipped with rolling eyes by the Waterbury Clock Company. Inanimate figures included ballplayers, horses, sunflowers, and Heaven knows what else.

One frequently sees nowadays old shelf clocks without dials or works which have been converted into wall cabinets. This is perhaps justified when one finds a clock with a well-designed case and the works in a state of helpless disrepair. But many people have a secret sense of discontent with these clock cabinets, as it is obvious what they were originally, and one cannot help regretting that they are no longer used for the purpose they were intended to serve. Also, it is not difficult to find a second clock with repairable works in an unhappily designed case. By transferring the works to the better case an assembled clock is created which is more desirable than fitting the good case with shelves and converting it into a cabinet.

Most people who enjoy restoring antiques like to tinker with old clocks. They are easily picked up at modest prices, and there is great satisfaction in restoring the case, replacing shattered glass, and repairing and cleaning the works. The last is the most difficult part of the operation, but if worse comes to worst and the clock cannot be made to run, it can always be taken to a professional clock man.

It may be wondered how the old clocks of New England have been kept going all these years, particularly in the hundreds of small towns which have never had a clockmaker. Most of these places have rarely been without some mechanically gifted Yankee who, among other things, understood old clocks and could put them right when they went wrong. Henry D. Thoreau seems to have been one of these, because when he and Ellery Channing visited Cape Cod and stayed with the old oysterman of Wellfleet they fixed his clock. "After breakfast," Thoreau wrote, "we looked at his clock, which was out of order, and oiled it with some 'hen's grease,' for want of sweet oil, for he could scarcely believe we were not tinkers or pedlers; meanwhile he told a story about visions, which had reference to a crack in the clock-case made by frost one night."

CABINET MAKER

10

Concerning Chests

THE celebrated Mayflower Compact, by which the Pilgrim Fathers combined themselves in "a civil body politick," was signed, according to tradition, on the lid of Elder Brewster's chest in the cabin of the *Mayflower*, while that vessel rode at anchor in Provincetown Harbor in November, 1620. This chest has for many years been in the possession of the Connecticut Historical Society in Hartford. It is a large, plain chest of yellow Norway pine stained brown, measuring four feet two inches long, one foot eight inches wide, and two feet six inches high. The key is so large that it has more the appearance of one belonging to an old-time prison than to a clothing receptacle. When new the chest must have been an inexpensive one, though now, of course, by reason of its associations, it is a priceless historical relic.

In the days when it was fashionable in Europe for people to keep dwarfs as we would keep a dog or a cat, the persons engaged in the trade of supplying fashionable people with these diminutive creatures sometimes resorted to the cruel practice of confining children in chests to stunt their growth. Collecting dwarfs was never a fad in this country, but it may be noted that one of Elder Brewster's descendants was a dwarf who might have occupied the ancestral chest with room to spare. This was the pretty, charming little creature Anna Brewster, whose height in womanhood was three feet. She was perfectly formed and had a sweet and intelligent face and an active mind. "Too little to be wooed, too wise to be won," says one historian, "she was loved and admired by everybody." As a girl she lived for a while at New Windsor, near Plattsburg, New York. When Washington had his headquarters there, Mrs. Washington was so taken with the sprightly little maiden that she invited her to visit her at the house where she and the general were quartered; but the invitation was declined, as it was felt that it had been extended out of curiosity rather than respect. This was a mistake, of course, but Anna Brewster was sensitive to inquisitiveness. She died in 1844, aged seventy-five. Fifty years before a rustic poet inspired by her charms during an evening passed in her company portrayed her character in the following verse:

ACROSTIC
A pretty, charming little creature,
N eat and complete in every feature,
N ow at New Windsor may be seen,
A ll beauteous in her air and mien.

Concerning Chests

<pre>
B irth and power, wealth and fame,
R ise not to view when her we name:
E very virtue in her shine,
W isely nice, but not o'er fine.
S he has a soul that's great, 'tis said,
T hough small's the body of this maid:
E 'en though the casket is but small,
R eason proclaims the jewel's all.
</pre>

* * *

The early settlers used chests as trunks in which to transport their personal belongings to the New World. It has frequently been stated that every Pilgrim who came over on the *Mayflower* probably had one. It may be so, but that overburdened craft measured only eighty-two feet over all, with a beam of twenty-two feet and a depth of fourteen feet. Crowded into this small ship were one hundred and two passengers and the crew. These, with the necessary provisions for the voyage, and the supplies and equipment indispensable to planting a new colony, must have taken up a large part of the space, leaving little room for a lot of chests the size of Elder Brewster's.

Yet during the first years thousands of chests were brought to this country from England and Holland. About 1640 the causes which inspired the early migrations no longer existed, and there was a sharp decline in the numbers who came to New England. But in the period between 1620 and 1640 some two hundred and ninety-eight ships brought 21,200 people, or about four thousand families. It is safe to say that every family had at least one chest, to say nothing of those belonging to the many single men seeking their fortunes in the New World.

A curious use to which one chest was put was for a coffin. A woman passenger on one of the ships that followed the *Mayflower* died at sea, just as the landfall of Cape Cod was made. They laid her in her chest and brought her ashore for burial. The funeral party was astonished when at the grave the lid of the improvised coffin suddenly flew open and the lady sat up in the box. The chest is cherished today by her descendants.

Chests were important pieces of furniture in colonial times. There were no closets in the first homes, and a chest was one of the few places a housewife had to keep linen, bedding, and clothing. As there were not many chairs, low chests were used for seats, while the higher ones served as tables. People also used to lie on them. The probate records for the middle decades of the seventeenth century show far more chests than tables and chairs.

Many colonial dames owned several chests. Alice Morse Earle cites the case of Jane Humphrey, who died in 1668 and in her will mentioned *my little chest, my great old chest, my great new chest, my lesser small box, my biggest small box*. And the men had them as well as the women. Thomas Wells of Ipswich, Massachusetts, by his will made in 1666, left his best chest to his wife. He likewise gave one to his son, and the planks to make another. *Also my will is, that every of these my Daughters, shall have each of them a Bible, & every of them a good chist.*

Concerning Chests

Although the early voyagers brought over many chests, it was not long before they were being made here by local joiners. Many fine examples produced during the last half of the seventeenth century have been found, particularly in the Connecticut Valley, especially in and around Hartford and Hadley. Dr. Irving W. Lyon, the great pioneer collector and early writer on antiques, lists the following types of New England chests: joined chests, wainscot chests, board chests, spruce chests, oak chests, ship chests, carved chests, chests with one and two drawers, and cypress chests.

The joined chests and the wainscot chests were much better made than the plain board chests. They were paneled framed chests, with the rails mortised into the corner posts, which also formed the legs. The uprights between the paneling were securely fastened into the rails, and the panels were fitted into the chest by means of grooved edges forming a rabbet joint. White oak was used throughout, except for the lid, the back, and the bottoms of the drawers, which were made of yellow pine. Red cedar was often employed for the decorative moldings of the front and ends. The knobs of the drawers were maple.

The two outstanding types of colonial oaken chests are the so-called Connecticut chest and the Hadley chest. Since about seventy-five of the former have been found in and around Hartford, they are sometimes called "Hartford chests." No two are exactly alike. Some have one long drawer underneath, others two, and some are without any. As a rule there are three carved panels across the front, though two-panel and even one-panel chests have been found. Most of them are of the two-drawer type, with three panels of quartered oak. All are approximately the same size, namely, forty inches high, forty-five inches long, and twenty-two inches wide. The local chest makers had a great advantage in being able to obtain large planks. There were giant trees in the New England forests then.

In the typical Connecticut chest, the three front panels are embellished with flat carving. The center panel is generally octagonal, the flanking panels square. The latter usually have a graceful tulip design, while the middle panel shows three sunflowers. This last feature has caused some people to refer to these chests as "sunflower chests." Each drawer front has two narrow panels with triangular corner pieces which give them an octagonal form. All the panels on the front and ends are framed in moldings of a contrasting wood, either stained cedar or pine painted red. A still wider molding between the drawers and also above and below them is painted black, as are the two oval bosses on each drawer panel. The shadow molding along the front top rail is similarly treated. On the corner posts of the upper part of the chest and on the stiles dividing the panels are flat-backed turned spindles or split balusters, with smaller ones on the posts at the ends of the drawers and in the middle between the drawer panels. These are also painted black. The idea behind this red-and-black decoration was to give the effect of rosewood and ebony, which were used at that time in the ornamentation of English and Dutch chests.

Concerning Chests

An interesting discovery was made a number of years ago by Dr. Luke Vincent Lockwood, the authority on colonial furniture. This was the finding of a fine example of a two-drawer Connecticut chest with the maker's name written on the back of one of the drawers. The inscription read *Mary Allyns Chistt Cutte and Joyned by Nich Disbrowe*.

With this as a clue, research revealed that Mary Allyn was the daughter of Colonel John Allyn, Colonial Secretary of Connecticut. Born in Hartford in 1657, she married William Whitney in 1686. Nicholas Disbrowe, who was born in Essex, England, came to this country at an early age. He served in the Hartford company of Captain John Mason in the expedition against the Pequots in 1637. In 1639 he was a property owner in Hartford, living in the north part of the town, where later he built a small joiner's shop. He died in 1683, leaving an estate of £210, a substantial sum for those days.

Apparently the chest was not signed by Disbrowe himself. On this point the late Henry W. Erving, the Hartford banker and antique collector, who owned several beautiful specimens of these chests, said:

> A very careful examination and comparison of the handwriting would indicate that this inscription was by the hand of John Allyn. The piece was probably a "dower chest" ordered and constructed for an adored baby girl—a common custom—and because of its beauty and excellence the father desired that the future owner should be informed as to its origin and share his admiration for the valuable article.

This Connecticut chest is believed to be the oldest piece of American furniture made by a workman whose name is known.

The Hadley chests were of the same order as the Hartford chests, which is not surprising, as Hadley, Massachusetts, was settled by Hartford people about 1660, following a religious dispute, which was often the cause of new towns being established. It is even possible that some of the joiners who made the Hadley chests may have served their apprenticeships in Hartford and learned to make chests there. John Allis, the leading chest maker of Hadley, was a relative of Nicholas Disbrowe. The Hadley chests are believed to have been produced during the last quarter of the seventeenth century and the first decade of the eighteenth. A delightful feature of these pieces comes from the custom of carving the initials of the owner in the center panel, thus making each chest unique.

No nails were used in framing the joined chests. The drawbore method was used in making the joints. A hole was bored through the sides of the mortises and through the tenons. These holes did not exactly correspond, so that when the square oaken pin was driven through them the tenons were drawn snugly into the mortises. Nails, however, were used to make the drawers and also to attach the oak cleats at the ends of the overhanging lid. Small brads and glue were employed in affixing the moldings and ornaments. All the hardware, nails and brads, hinges and locks, were made at the village smithy. If the upper part of the chest locked, the drawers were secured by boring a hole down through them and inserting a long pin. That the chests were used for valuables, as well as for linen, bedding, and clothing, is shown by the presence in most of them of a covered till at one end.

The English oaken chests of this period are distinguished by their all-oak construction and the fact that the wood used was darker than the white oak of New England.

Another type of early New England chest was the so-called Taunton chest, which was made during the first half of the eighteenth century at Taunton, Massachusetts. It was a painted chest. As in the case of the carved Connecticut chest, the tulip was a favorite decorative motif. One usually associates this flower with the folk art of the Pennsylvania Germans, who made effective use of it on their dower chests and many other things besides, but it was used in New England long before there were any of these people in Pennsylvania.

Sea chests are dealt with elsewhere in this book, but it may be mentioned here that they were sold along the water fronts and were generally called "slop chests." "Slops" were cheap ready-made clothing. Among seamen the term was also applied to bedding, etc. Most sea chests are distinguished by rope handles through which the lines passed by which they were lashed to the deck.

Popular as they were at first, chests were actually rather inconvenient, because, as everybody knows who has ever used one, the thing wanted has a habit of always being at the bottom where it has to be dug out. It was to avoid this that a long drawer was added underneath, but as one was not enough a second drawer soon appeared. Further drawers were added, until by the beginning of the eighteenth century the hinged top had vanished altogether and the old chest with drawers became a chest of drawers. Then there was the chest-on-chest, which was actually two chests of drawers, one placed on top of the other. To add to its usefulness, one of the drawer fronts was sometimes made to let down to provide a place to write. But all this did not put an end to the making of chests. An old pine chest picked up by the writer looks as if it were a chest of drawers, but the two upper drawers are cleverly made fakes and the lid lifts up to reveal the true nature of the piece—a blanket chest.

About this same time, to save bending over, the chest of drawers was placed on a frame with six legs, four in front and two in the rear, connected and strengthened all around by stretchers just above the feet. Thus the highboy was evolved from the chest. The early ones had flat tops, but presently the hooded top appeared, followed by the famous broken arch. Two of the front legs were eliminated, only pendants showing where they had been. Cherry and maple were favored by the New England cabinetmakers for highboys.

Toward the end of the eighteenth century and the early part of the nineteenth a good deal of furniture was made in the various Shaker communities scattered through New England. These religionists sought perfection in everything. Honesty of craftsmanship they considered a moral duty, and the integrity of their work may be seen in the simple chests and other pieces of furniture which they made. They did not try to conceal

Concerning Chests

the dovetailing at the corners of their chests, because that would have been deceitful. Nor did they, being a plain sect like the Quakers, believe in decorating or ornamenting their furniture in any way. Apart from ornamentation being a worldly vanity, they feared it might interfere with the purity of the design, perhaps even hide defects in it. No Shaker craftsman would have dreamed of carving or painting a chest after the fashion of the Hartford, Hadley, or Taunton chests. Everything was kept as plain and severe and functional as possible and for this reason the Shaker chests and other furniture possess a modern look which has a special attraction for people today.

Iron chests, forerunners of the modern safe, with great keys to turn the heavy locks, were not altogether unknown in colonial New England. Doubtless they provided a certain measure of protection against fire and theft. When one of the large old chest keys turns up in a curiosity shop, it has been known to be labeled KEY TO THE BASTILLE and sold as a historical relic.

"I won't guarantee its genuineness," says the dealer, "but that's the story as I got it."

These French Revolutionary keys bring to mind the bathtub in which Charlotte Corday murdered Marat. Not so long ago five were sold in this country in one year, each complete with the authentic bloodstains.

Another kind of chest that figured in a famous historical episode was the tea chest. In the Old South Meeting House in Boston there is a glass phial containing some of the original tea thrown into the harbor at the time of the Boston Tea Party. It was in this same church that the meeting of the patriots took place just before a party of them disguised as Indians went down to Griffin's Wharf and boarded the tea ships. In less than two hours this strange band of Indians staved in and emptied two hundred and forty chests of tea and one hundred half chests. Although a sample of the tea was saved, apparently none of the chests escaped being used for kindling wood.

Although a fair number of old chests have survived, many more have perished. The very places where some have been found is an indication of the fate that has overtaken great numbers of them. Relegated to barns, cellars, and sheds when they had outlived their usefulness in the house and put to rough uses they were never intended to serve, or simply left to decay in some damp or unprotected place, many stout old chests have gone to pieces. For a while, when the demand for them was greater than it is today, the New England dealers sold many chests that were brought down from Canada. Not so many are sold now, though a good chest which has withstood the ravages of time is always worth owning.

CHAIR MAKER

II

Chairs

THERE were few chairs in New England in the early days. People sat on stools, on forms or benches, and on chests. They must have been uncomfortable, but the scarcity of chairs was not because of any desire to mortify the flesh, nor to poverty, nor to difficulties of transportation. It was because chairs were not much in favor at the time. Even in England they were seldom seen in ordinary homes.

The chairs which the colonists did have were ponderous affairs and, except for the support they gave the sitter's back, did little to ease the seating situation until well along in the seventeenth century. Colonial furniture, indeed, gives one the impression that the early settlers were literally a strait-laced people.

The three types of chairs most in use during the Pilgrim century were the turned chair, the wainscot chair, and the Cromwellian chair, with a leather or textile seat and back. Good specimens of the turned type are the high-backed chairs of Governor Carver and Elder Brewster in Pilgrim Hall, Plymouth. Large, massive, and masculine, they are composed entirely of turnings fitted together. The Carver chair is the simpler one of the two, the Brewster chair having turned spindles not only in the back, but also under the arms and between the stretchers at the front and sides below the seat. Although Governor Carver and Elder Brewster doubtless looked quite dignified sitting in their great chairs, they could have taken little comfort in them.

Another example of the turned type is the president's chair at Harvard. This famous triangular seat is a fussy piece of furniture loaded with such a profusion of turnery as to suggest the days of Victoria rather than those of Charles. Oliver Wendell Holmes describes it in a ballad called "Parson Turell's Legacy; or, the President's Old Arm-Chair," which he inserted in *The Autocrat at the Breakfast Table*.

> Funny old chair with seat like wedge,
> Sharp behind and broad front edge,—
> One of the oddest human things,
> Turned all over with knobs and rings,—
> But heavy, and wide, and deep, and grand,—
> Fit for the worthies of the land.

Different woods were used in the early turned chairs. Ash was always employed for the substantial front and back posts, hickory as a rule for the arms and stretchers. The spindles in the back were often of birch. The seats were generally made of rushes, though the inner fibrous bark of the elm and the bass or linden tree was also sometimes used for this purpose.

The wainscot chairs were invariably made of oak and were extremely heavy, as they had solid wooden seats and backs and were sometimes boxed in beneath the seat. The backs were frequently paneled and carved. Occasionally the paneling matched that of the room in which the chair stood, but oftener it was more like that seen on cupboards and chests. Perhaps the best known of these chairs is the one in Pilgrim Hall named for its owner, "The Winslow Chair."

Carved wainscot chairs were costly and were to be found only in the homes of people of means and standing in the community. Sometimes the date appears in the decoration on the back. The story is told of an antique dealer who had the date 1635 and a coat-of-arms carved on the back of a genuine old wainscot chair, in an attempt to enhance its value. Unfortunately for him, the fraud was detected because the coat-of-arms he chose to have reproduced had not been granted until nearly a century after the date on the chair.

The high-backed settles, which, as everybody knows, were designed to keep draughts off people while they sat beside the fire in winter, likewise had paneled backs. Some were provided with a small bracket shelf, affixed to the middle of the back, which was just large enough to hold a candlestick at a convenient height for reading.

Probably the most comfortable of the seventeenth-century chairs was the low-backed Cromwellian with its leather or Turkey-work seat and back. Wealthy families frequently had sets of these chairs. As in the case of the turned and the wainscot chair, some were imported from England, others made in America. Before the end of the century most of the population of New England were sitting on chairs, though not wholly without discomfort.

It was not until the early decades of the eighteenth century that the easy chair made its appearance. This was the upholstered wing chair, which was first used in bedrooms. It was sometimes covered with the same material as the bed and window curtains. Salt marsh hay was used in stuffing many of these chairs. This was such a comfortable chair that it soon emerged from the seclusion of the bedchamber and became part of the living-room furniture. It has numerous descendants today, most of them showing some family resemblance.

Other chairs common in colonial New England were the chair with the cane seat and back, the bandy-leg or bow-leg chair, the banister-back and the roundabout, the slat-back and the Windsor. Most of these were copies of English types, or were suggested by them. The bandy-leg chair seems to have been Dutch. It frequently had the claw-and-ball foot, sometimes described in probate inventories as "eaglesfoot" and "crowfoot." Occasionally the shell on the knee is also mentioned in the old records. Dr. Lyon says the claw-and-ball foot originated in China, where for centuries the motif of the dragon grasping a pearl was used.

The banister-back chair is found with and without arms. Tall and generally narrow, it took its name from the vertical spindles, usually four in number, set into the frame of the back. These were turned like stair banisters, save for the flat front side, against which the sitter leaned. The turned front legs, with Flemish or Spanish feet, were joined by a bulbous stretcher. The turned back posts were topped with knobs, and the back was crested in a variety of pleasing ways. Although provided with a rush or splint seat, the banister-back was never remarkable for comfort. It was a rather sophisticated chair, and though quantities were made of maple, ash, and pine, and it was seen everywhere, the bandy-leg was largely a parlor piece.

The roundabout chair with the arms and legs forming a continuous curve of the same height, except perhaps for a top piece on the back, came in during the first part of the eighteenth century. The better ones were made of walnut, mahogany, and cherry. It was a comfortable species of armchair, and the idea of the curving back and arms was embodied later in the so-called barroom or captain's chair.

An odd piece of dual-purpose furniture was the chair table, which generally had a round top, but sometimes a square or rectangular one. When this piece of furniture was used as a table, the top rested on the arms of the chair, but when the top was tilted up into a vertical position—it turned on wooden pins at the junction of the arms with the back posts—it formed the back of a chair, which usually stood against the wall. This curious form of furniture was first used in New England about the middle of the seventeenth century and is still made. The early ones were generally of oak and pine and had no drawer under the seat, as have the later chair tables.

The familiar slat-back, which had anywhere from two to six horizontal back pieces curved to fit the sitter's back, and the no less well-known Windsor, which came in various styles, were enormously popular for many years. But the two most characteristic New England chairs were the Hitchcock chair and the Boston rocker. They were the bestsellers of the furniture trade of yesteryear.

The village of Hitchcocksville, now Riverton, where Lambert Hitchcock made the chairs which have immortalized his name, is on the West Branch of the Farmington River in the township of Barkhamsted, Connecticut. The village lies along both sides of the river amid typical New England surroundings of hills, woods, and rocks. At one end of the bridge which spans the river stands the old brick chair factory with its square cupola topped by a weathervane, while facing it at the other end is the still older Riverton Inn with two porches, one above the other, extending across its front. The inn, known in Hitchcock's time as "The Ives Tavern," dates from 1800, the chair works from 1826. "Rest for the Weary" could appropriately have been used by the proprietors of both places for a trade slogan.

Lambert Hitchcock was a Connecticut Yankee, but not a native of Barkhamsted. Descended from pioneer New Haven stock, he was born in Cheshire, June 28, 1795. When he was six, his father, who had fought in the Revolution, met a tragic fate at sea. In 1818, at the age of twenty-three, Lambert moved to Barkhamsted, where he began to manufacture chair parts. Among the considerations which may have led the youthful cabinetmaker to choose such a small, out-of-the-way place for his factory were ample local supplies of wood suitable for chairmaking and the water power of the Farmington River.

The business prospered from the first. New England at that time manufactured largely for the Southern market, and Lambert Hitchcock shipped thousands of chair parts to seaboard cities and other business centers in the South, where the chairs were assembled. Many were also sold to the Yankee peddlers who infested the region. They bought the parts and put them together themselves as they needed them. Shipment from Connecticut to the South was by coastwise sailing vessels, chiefly through the river port of Hartford, twenty-six miles from Hitchcocksville.

At the time Hitchcock launched his business, the American Windsor chair, which originated in Philadelphia and enjoyed a long run, was being pushed aside by newer styles coming into the market. So was the old slat-back, or ladder-back, chair. The Hitchcock soon superseded all others in popularity. It remained the favorite for many years, until at length it was, in turn, displaced, by the Empire style.

Whether or not Lambert Hitchcock originated the chair which bears his name is not definitely known, but he may very well have done so, or at least have been responsible for certain of its distinctive features. In any case, there is no question that his chairs are among the finest of the so-called Hitchcock type, and his designs are followed today by those who still make them.

Although engaged in what was called the "fancy chair" trade, Hitchcock's productions were actually quite simple. The typical Hitchcock chair is nothing but a straight chair with a rush or cane seat, or even a wooden one, broader at the front than at the back, and with the front edge rounded for the comfort of the sitter. The front legs and the front rung are turned, while the others are plain. The back legs extend above the seat to form the uprights of the back, which at the top are flat and curve backward slightly. They are joined by a turned top rail, usually in what is called the "pillow-top" design, which seems to have been derived from Sheraton, or by a flat, arched toppiece similar to that seen on Boston rockers. A wide, curved, horizontal back slat, often with a narrow slat below it, is another feature. The back slat takes many different forms, from the simple straight one to the "turtle" back, the "button" back, the "crown" back, and other designs. It is on this back slat that the principal decoration of the chair is centered—the stenciled horns of plenty, baskets of fruit or flowers, clusters of grapes, and other conventional designs, including a fountain with birds refreshing themselves.

These chairs were not made for any luxury market, but were cheap furniture produced in quantity for the ordinary American household in town and country. Yet they were strongly built of the best wood procurable, usually birch or maple. They were light and sturdy and that they were made to last is shown by the number which have survived after years of service. In one Connecticut farmhouse attic with which I am familiar are eight or ten of these chairs, most of them differing from each other in some detail of decoration or design. They

Chairs

are held in reserve and brought down when the family returns in force for a holiday gathering. Four or five generations of the family have used them.

When Lambert Hitchcock settled in Barkhamsted, few people were living in the northwest corner of the town where he established his business. About a mile downstream were the cabins of an Indian village, occupied by a remnant of the Narragansett tribe, a score or two in number, who had purchased a couple of hundred acres in the valley. The opening of the chair factory soon attracted settlers and by 1821 the thriving community which sprang up around it was known as "Hitchcocksville," a name it retained until 1866, when "Hitchcocksville" was changed to "Riverton" because it was frequently confused with Hotchkissville.

The making and selling of chair parts was continued for only the first few years, and was then abandoned in favor of manufacturing finished chairs. This gave employment to whole families. The men did the woodwork, operating the saws, lathes, and finishing machines, while the women and children painted and decorated the chairs. The children put on the primary coat of Venetian red, which on old chairs can sometimes be seen showing through the black coat the women painted over it. Then came the stenciling, which was also done by the women. Using paper stencils, they laid in the groundwork by dipping their fingers in oil, then in gold, bronze, or silver powder, and applying it to the stencil. The spots of color which pricked out the design were added afterward with a brush, as were also the touches of gold on the turnings of the legs and the uprights of the back. Mabel Roberts Moore, whose monograph on Hitchcock chairs is the best thing on the subject, says the fingers of the women who did the stenciling became as hard as boards.

There is no doubt that the attractive decoration helped greatly to promote the sale of the Hitchcock line of chairs. Their popularity, indeed, increased at such a rate that in 1826, less than ten years after he entered the chair business, Lambert Hitchcock was able to build the brick factory building which still stands on the bank of the Farmington River. In this plant, employing upwards of a hundred hands, he turned out fifteen thousand chairs annually. These included, in addition to many different styles of his straight chair, a number of children's chairs and a variety of rockers.

The rocking chair is an American invention, but who the inventor was nobody knows. There is a legend that Benjamin Franklin was the first to put rockers on a chair. A visitor to Philadelphia after the Revolution reported seeing an old slat-back chair mounted on rockers in his home. But long before that they were adding rockers to chairs in the Connecticut Valley, and the evidence points to New England as the place of origin. Walter A. Dyer thinks the first one came from Connecticut. In any case, the Boston rocker was the most popular of them all, and Lambert Hitchcock is believed to have been the first to manufacture this chair in quantity.

The rocking chair is in exile today, but forty years ago it was to be seen in every home. Whether the idea for the chair was derived from the cradle or not, millions of Americans now living can remember being lulled to sleep in infancy in the old family rocking chair. As one who was brought up in that period, I was familiar with rockers. I recall one that creaked dreadfully when in motion. Another that was my grandmother's had very short rockers extending only a few inches beyond the legs, which made it an excitingly tippy chair, and there was one with long sweeping rockers over which I tumbled and beneath which I had my toes pinched more than once. Still another, a triumph of the eighties or nineties, was an upholstered patented chair equipped with springs and a stationary wooden base on which the rockers rested.

People then sat and rocked not only inside their homes, but also outside on their porches in specially made outdoor rockers. In late spring a familiar sight on the streets of New England cities were the long open wagons of the furniture peddlers, loaded with veranda chairs and brightly painted garden benches, many of the pieces hanging from the framework that was erected on the vehicles. These peddlers did business in the residential streets.

The so-called Cape Cod rocker was a long bench with a demountable rail across part of the front to keep an infant lying on the seat from rolling off. The Cape Cod served the dual purpose of a rocker and a cradle. A mother could sit and knit or otherwise occupy herself and at the same time rock herself and her baby. Hitchcock sold his Cape Cod rockers, which were painted and decorated like his other chairs, for forty cents a foot, a six-footer selling for only two dollars and forty cents. All of these rockers he continued to produce as long as he was in the furniture business. There is a tradition that before Lambert Hitchcock made rocking chairs it was only possible to buy the rockers separately, to put on already existing chairs.

The Boston rocker, which Wallace Nutting thinks was the most popular chair ever made in America, was produced at the Hitchcocksville factory beginning in the eighteen-twenties, when it first appeared. Lambert Hitchcock had previously experimented with rocking chairs. He had put rockers on a high-backed version of his own chair, to which he added arms. This had the flat seat and the turnings and decorations of the straight Hitchcock, but it was an ungainly-looking thing, and the rarity of the chair today is an indication that not many were made. Turning to the Boston rocker, he began to make not only the true type of this chair, but also the little Boston without arms, and a child's Boston.

Who made the first Boston rocker is not known. It seems to have just suddenly appeared about the end of the first quarter of the nineteenth century. It promptly swept the country and marked the beginning of the rocking-chair era. It was an altered form of the Windsor chair, but whereas the Windsor was usually painted green, the Boston was generally black with stenciling on the wide top rail. The seat, which curved up in the back and down in front, was as a rule made of several pieces of pine. Ash, hickory, maple, or oak was used for the legs and spindles. There was nothing beautiful about the chair, but it was extremely comfortable, and its popularity helped to bring prosperity to Lambert Hitchcock.

But it was not all fair sailing for this enterprising Connecticut Yankee. He sold his chairs for a dollar and a half apiece, but he had great difficulty collecting the money owed him. Competitors copied his line and undersold him. In the summer of 1829, following repeated losses and misfortunes, he found himself unable to meet his obligations, amounting to over twenty thousand dollars, and was compelled to make an assignment for the benefit of his creditors. Among his assets, he listed fifteen hundred chairs at the factory in Hitchcocksville, another fifteen hundred in Hartford, five hundred in New Haven, and many more in various markets in different parts of the country. He also had quantities of stock, machinery, and tools for the manufacture of chairs, including lumber, paints, oil, cane, and rushes. Mention of material in the hands of the warden of the state's prison at Wethersfield shows that he used some convict labor, probably for making the rush and cane seats. It also appeared that Hitchcock was a partner in a general store which had recently burned. His personal library, which was sold for the benefit of the creditors, included a number of classics.

The four trustees to whom Hitchcock assigned his property took over the business, but he ran it as their agent and in three years succeeded in working his way out of his financial difficulties. In November, 1832, he announced in the *Hartford Courant* that he had resumed the business on his own account and responsibility, adding that he had on hand "a large and elegant assortment of chairs, made after the latest fashions, and finished in the best manner."

Across the back strip of the seat on all his chairs Hitchcock had his name and guarantee stenciled in gold, L. HITCHCOCK, HITCHCOCKSVILLE, CONNECTICUT. WARRANTED. This meant that the chair was well and honestly made of carefully selected materials. The stencil was changed in 1832, when Hitchcock took the superintendent of his plant, Arba Alford, Junior, into partnership, so that it read, HITCHCOCK, ALFORD & Co. WARRANTED.

Two years earlier Hitchcock, despite the financial crisis through which he was passing, had married Eunice Alford, the sister of the man who became his partner. With the return of prosperity, the two brothers-in-law built a spacious double house across the way from the chair factory. The old brick place, with its solid wooden pillars, is still standing and is owned by a descendant of Arba Alford.

The new partnership worked well. Alford had charge of the factory, while Hitchcock traveled far and wide selling the output. That the latter was a good salesman and covered an extensive territory is plain from the wide distribution the chairs received. They turn up everywhere. Hitchcock journeyed by land and sea, afoot and on horseback, in stagecoaches, canalboats, and sailing vessels. To be within easier reach of the centers of trade, he and his wife moved to Hartford in 1834, and that same year he was elected to represent Barkhamsted in the Connecticut Legislature. In 1840 and 1841 he served as State senator. While on one of his selling trips in December, 1841, he tarried a few days in Washington, visiting the United States Senate and calling at the

White House, where he met the President and Mrs. Tyler.

Soon after this the Hitchcock and Alford partnership was dissolved and Hitchcock moved to Unionville, where he carried on the chair business by himself, making the same old line, which now bore the mark LAMBERT HITCHCOCK, UNIONVILLE, CONNECTICUT.

In 1835 Eunice Hitchcock had died at the age of thirty, and the following year Lambert Hitchcock married Mary Preston at Cazenovia, New York, by whom he had three sons and a daughter. Then in 1852 he died. At his request his ex-partner, Arba Alford, was made executor of his estate. Although Lambert Hitchcock has a place in *Webster's Dictionary,* he is not included in the *Dictionary of American Biography.* No picture of the Yankee chairmaker seems to have survived.

Arba Alford, with his brother Alfred as partner, continued to make chairs at Hitchcocksville under the firm name of Alford & Company, until the Civil War pretty much ruined the business. The factory was sold during the war to Leroy and Delos Stephens, who manufactured pocket rulers there until about the turn of the century. For a while the plant was used as a rubber works for the manufacture of sundries for the drug trade. Then after a period of vacancy the historic factory was reopened a year or two ago by John T. Kenney and Richard Coombs, for the production of Hitchcock chairs true in every detail to the famous originals of more than a century ago, even to the stencil L. HITCHCOCK, HITCHCOCKSVILLE, CONN. WARRANTED.

MERCHANT

12

A Silvery Metal Called Pewter

PEOPLE have been doing things for ages with the gray-hued silvery metal called "pewter." An alloy composed principally of tin, it is the oldest composite metal known. It is so old, indeed, that nobody knows when or where it originated. Although pewter is a base metal, lacking the glamour and intrinsic value of the precious metals, old pewter pieces have by reason of their sturdy character and quiet, unpretentious simplicity cast a spell over the modern collector.

It probably never occurred to the early craftsman in the metal, working to meet the demands of his time, that the simple functional articles which he cast and hammered and polished would come to be regarded as things of artistic merit and find honored places in public and private collections. Striving to produce household utensils and other things which in size and form were best suited to serve the purpose for which they were intended, the pewterer endeavored at the same time to maintain a well-balanced relationship between line and proportion. That he succeeded is shown by many surviving pieces which bear favorable comparison with the best work of the silversmiths.

New England was the center of the pewter trade in America during the period when the ware was in common use everywhere. It was extremely popular and highly esteemed. John Hancock loved it; he abhorred the clatter of china dishes. A person who owned a "garnish" of pewter, as a collection of flatware was called, was proud of it. A garnish consisted of thirty-six pieces, a dozen each of three different sizes of tableware, namely, twelve chargers or large plates, twelve shallow basins or dishes, and twelve small plates. Kept bright and shining, these usually stood on edge along the rear of the dresser shelves, where they formed a background for other pewter designed for table use, such as tankards, mugs, and beakers, and for the rows of pewter porringers hanging by their handles from hooks along the front of the shelves.

Besides these articles, many other table accessories were made of pewter, including teapots and coffeepots, sugar bowls and creamers, pepper and mustard pots, salts, jugs, pitchers, spoons, and ladles. A prodigious number of pewter candlesticks, candle molds, and tinder boxes were made and sold and later many whale-oil and camphine lamps. Inkwells and trays were produced in quantity, as were also such items of personal adornment as buckles for shoes and hats and all sizes of buttons. Barbers' basins with a section cut out of the rim for

A Silvery Metal Called Pewter

compassing a man's neck and shaving mugs were also part of the output of the pewter shops. An amazing number of things were made from the metal.

Yet in spite of the extensive use to which it was put, relatively little old pewter is now extant. It is unusual to meet with it in any quantity or variety outside museums and private collections. The reason so much perished was because pewter is not a very durable metal. If placed near the fire it melts in a short time, and prolonged exposure to dampness and cold causes it to disintegrate. It bends and dents easily and constant cleaning wears it out. Tinkers used to do a thriving business going about the countryside repairing damaged pewter and recasting spoons. Furthermore, during the Revolution a great deal of pewter was melted down and cast into bullets for the Continental Army, patriotic housewives sacrificing their best pieces and using woodenware instead.

It was at this time that a pewter dish filled with succotash was the cause of a British general having an experience which he probably never forgot. In Lebanon, Connecticut, nearly opposite the mansion of Governor Trumbull—Brother Jonathan, as Washington called him —stood the old tavern kept during the Revolution by Captain Alden. It was famous as the house where General Prescott, the tyrannical British officer in command of the enemy occupation forces in Rhode Island, stopped to dine. In the summer of 1777, Colonel William Barton of the patriot army boldly kidnaped the general near Newport and it was when the prisoner was on his way under guard to Washington's camp in New

Jersey that he paused at Lebanon. While General Prescott was seated at the table, Mrs. Alden brought him some succotash of her own making in a pewter dish. But the general was unappreciative. Evidently unaccustomed to such food, he looked at it and was furious.

"What?" he cried indignantly. "Do you treat me with the food of hogs?"

And seizing the dish he strewed the contents on the floor and flung the pewter container in the midst of the mess. Nonplussed by the officer's conduct, Mrs. Alden retreated hastily from the room and told her husband, who entered immediately with a horsewhip and gave the general a sound thrashing.

Most of the early pewter used in America came from England. With the exception of part of a spoon unearthed a few years ago at Jamestown, Virginia, with the mark on it of Joseph Copeland, who worked at Chuckatuck, Virginia, from 1675 to 1691, no piece of pewter of native origin made before 1700 is known to exist. Yet there were pewterers at work in New England soon after the establishment of the first settlements. In 1635 Robert Graves was casting pewter at Salem and a few years later several others are known to have been engaged in the trade in Massachusetts. But for many years the bulk of the pewter sold in this country continued to be imported from England.

In 1720 Judge Sewall ordered from London a long list of house furnishings for his daughter, Judith, who was about to be married. Besides such items as a fine large chintz quilt, a good large warming pan, and a pair of bellows with brass noses, the list included *One Duzen* of large *hard-mettal Pewter Plates new fashion, weighing about fourteen pounds,* and *One Duzen hard-mettal Pewter Porringers.* The weight of the plates was mentioned because flatware was commonly sold by the pound.

The Worshipful Company of Pewterers, one of the oldest and most powerful guilds in London, was opposed to any pewter being made in America, because the market here was an important outlet for its wares. This fitted in with British colonial policy. For while England was anxious to receive supplies of certain raw materials from the New World, it aimed at protecting its home industries and did all it could to discourage manufacturing of all kinds in the colonies. It was in a strong position as far as pewter was concerned, as America was dependent on the mines of Cornwall for its supplies of tin, the basic element of pewter. It was a simple matter for the government to place a heavy duty on the metal in block, and at the same time permit it to be freely exported in the form of finished pewter ware.

But the American pewterers were undismayed. They bought up quantities of old discarded pewter and this scrap was melted down and recast. The market for used pewter became so brisk that merchants cheerfully accepted worn-out and broken pieces in exchange for merchandise.

By 1758, the industry here had grown to such an extent that the Worshipful Company, thoroughly alarmed, endeavored to stop the sale to America of the molds used for casting pewter. The Worshipful Company had no jurisdiction over American pewterers, nor was there any organization corresponding to it in this country which could insist on the high standards maintained by the Worshipful Company in London. This meant that English pewter had to compete in the American market with a cheaper grade of native metal. During the troublesome times that preceded the Revolution pewter made in England was among the things the people of Boston resolved to boycott.

For many years an enormous gilt teapot with steam issuing from its spout has hung over the entrance to a teashop in Scollay Square in Boston. The capacity of the pot is painted on its side—227 GALLONS, 2 QUARTS, 1 PINT, 3 GILLS. When the shop first opened at another location on the square there was a guessing contest as to how much it held. A much earlier giant Boston teakettle was that of Henry Shrimpton, the wealthy colonial merchant, who had one on top of his house. He was a prosperous pewterer who made and sold quantities of pewter ware to the colonists. It was an ancient and honorable calling to which Shrimpton was proud to belong. So when he retired from business he had the mammoth teapot placed on his roof to indicate the line of trade in which he had made a fortune.

A person wishing to set up shop as a pewterer required little equipment, but it was expensive, especially the molds. Pewter was cast in the desired form and then finished with hand tools. After the casting had been removed from the mold it was trimmed, surface defects were remedied, and the rough piece filed smooth. It was then polished on a lathe. Small articles were cast in one piece, large articles in two or more pieces which were soldered together. It sounds as if it were a simple enough process, but it took a good deal of knowledge and skill to make all but the simplest things, and apprentices to the pewter trade served seven years.

Pewter is an easy metal to work. Composed principally of tin, copper, antimony, and bismuth, with occasionally an admixture of lead, it melts at from 400 to 500 degrees Fahrenheit, depending on the mixture used, as against 1830 degrees for silver. No set formula for making the alloy has ever been universally followed. In this country the purpose for which an article was made governed the composition of the metal. In the early days a good deal of lead was used, but even then it was recognized that the less lead the better the pewter and the best grade contained none. Owing to the danger of lead poisoning the amount which could be used was strictly regulated by the Worshipful Company, and the best English and American craftsmen followed more or less closely the formulas and rules established at Pewterers' Hall. Articles not designed for eating or drinking, such as candle molds and candlesticks, often had a high lead content. The dullness and heaviness of many old pieces is attributable to the presence of a large percentage of lead in the alloy.

Because of its low melting point pewter could be cast in almost any kind of mold—clay, stone, wood, iron, brass, gun-metal, bronze, etc. But plaster was good for only one casting, and sand molds did not last long. When sand was used it was often moistened with stale beer or ale. The New England Indians were quick to master the art of making the bright pewter buttons they liked, carving molds for this purpose in soapstone. It is related that in one town a family which had a spoon mold used to lend it to the neighbors, with the result that all the spoons in that vicinage bore the same initial. Although small brass molds have been used successfully, bronze has proved the best material for permanent molds. These were very expensive and were handed down from father to son.

The high cost of the molds restricted the variety of pieces that could be turned out and hence less diversity of shape is to be found in pewter than in silver. Nor was the casting method so well adapted to surface ornamentation. But the pewterers often succeeded in giving pieces as graceful lines and pleasing proportions as the silversmiths.

Many of the forms which pewter took in New England were traditionally English, but the native craftsmen were not content to follow these patterns closely, and developed distinctive designs of their own. Take porringers, for example. They were popular in this country for some time after the European pewterers stopped making them. The market for them continued, indeed, until the last few decades of the pewter era, which ended in 1850. The basic types followed here were the solid-handled continental type and the openwork English type. From these two types different patterns were evolved. This was done with notable success by the pewterers of Newport and Providence, whose work was so distinctive that collectors now speak of the Rhode Island handle.

The Boston pewterers seem to have specialized largely

in flatware. They made well-finished plates of high-grade pewter which are distinguishable as a rule by their shallowness and narrow edges. They made other forms of pewter, too, but there is a paucity of identifiable specimens. Quart mugs by Nathaniel Austin of Charlestown, whose principal work was done in the eighteenth century, and by George Richardson of Boston, who was active in the nineteenth, have been spotted, but nothing else.

The third great pewter region of New England was the Connecticut Valley. All kinds of pewter ware was made here, chiefly by the Danforth dynasty of pewterers, who go back to Thomas Danforth of Norwich. A dozen or more of his descendants were in the business, the family carrying on for more than a century. Old Thomas Danforth (1703–1786) is one of the best known colonial pewterers. His work is highly esteemed by collectors. He came from England and on landing at Boston went directly to Taunton. After tarrying there for a while, he moved to Norwich, Connecticut, where he worked until his retirement in 1773, following a successful career during which he trained a number of apprentices in the art of making pewter.

Of his descendants, the Boardman brothers of Hartford were the most prolific producers of pewter. Their mother was Sarah Danforth, a granddaughter of the original Thomas. Thomas Danforth Boardman was born in Litchfield January 21, 1784, and died September 10, 1873. His brother Sherman Boardman was born in Litchfield July 10, 1787, and died March 20, 1861. About 1804 Thomas Danforth Boardman began the manufacture of pewter on Main Street in Hartford and continued the business with his brother for almost half a century. The Boardmans and other Connecticut Valley pewterers were skillful and versatile, as the many different examples of their work which have survived attest. The ecclesiastical pewter which they made is considered particularly fine.

Many town and country Churches in New England which could not afford silver Communion services used pewter sets. Complete sets could be bought, but more often than not they were assembled piece by piece, either by gift or purchase, as is shown by the presence in the same set of vessels bearing the marks of different makers. While some pewter was made expressly for ecclesiastical purposes, such as flagons, chalices, and beakers, many sets were composed entirely of domestic pieces. A complete Communion service did not consist of any specific number of pieces, but varied more or less according to the size of the congregation. The wine was poured from a flagon or tankard, and a set usually included a pair or several pairs of goblet-shaped chalices, which take high rank for beauty of form among examples of American-made pewter; a number of beakers or simple drinking cups, and several patens. Pewter baptismal bowls and collection plates were also used by the New England Churches.

Old records disclose that when the Church in Hanover, Massachusetts, purchased a pewter Communion service in 1728, the three tankards cost ten shillings apiece, the five beakers six shillings and a sixpence each, and the two platters five shillings apiece. When a

Church acquired a silver service it sometimes gave its old pewter set to some less wealthy congregation, which was perhaps using wooden vessels.

The oddest pieces of ecclesiastical pewter are the Communion tokens or checks. These small oblong disks, about an inch or an inch and a half long, were used when joint Communion services were held by a number of congregations. Church societies without a settled minister, or during the absence of their regular pastor, would combine with a society having an ordained minister to commemorate the Lord's Supper. Sometimes hundreds of communicants from several parishes would assemble in one church for this purpose. To make certain that no unworthy person should partake of the sacrament, the deacons gave checks to the members of their congregations in good standing, who had to present them before they were allowed to take Communion.

In New Hampshire, the Presbyterian Churches around Londonderry followed the old Scotch custom and met twice a year for joint Communion services in the Londonderry church. Tokens were used at these convocations as late as the year 1830. The checks were stamped with the letters "L.D.," but what they stood for is not known, though it has been suggested that it may have been "Lord's Day" or "Londonderry."

The Scotch-Irish Presbyterians of the hilltop town of Pelham, Massachusetts, had what was perhaps a unique system of tokens. During the month the deacons gave checks to "deserving" persons and withheld them from those they deemed unworthy. On Communion Sunday only those holding tokens were permitted to receive the sacrament. This system, which gave the deacons the practical power of excommunication, was installed late in the eighteenth century by the notorious ministerial imposter Stephen Burroughs, whose later crimes included counterfeiting. The pewter checks used were marked "P.P.," which it is supposed stood for "Pelham Presbyterian."

To the collectors of old pewter the maker's mark, or "touch," is of primary importance. The American pewter trade, although under no compulsion to do so, followed the English system of marking much of its output. A knowledge of these marks often enables one to tell when, where, and by whom a piece was made, as there are lists of pewterers giving the period and place where each worked. Steel dies were used by the pewterers to impress their marks on their output, a piece being struck after it had been removed from the mold and cooled. Small dies were used for small articles, large dies for large pieces. The marks, which appear in relief, take a variety of forms, some makers using their names, others their initials, and some just a symbol; but the usual practice was to use the name or initials in a distinctive design, often in combination with a symbol. Some pewterers used a series of small hallmarks in imitation of the silversmiths, though silversmiths were sometimes also pewterers. Paul Revere worked in both metals.

Before the Revolution the British lion and the figure of Britannia were popular American marks, as was also the rose and crown, which was used by both English and French pewterers. A tiny crown above an "X" was

A Silvery Metal Called Pewter

employed in Great Britain and in this country to indicate pewter of a superior quality. Sometimes the X was used without the crown. After the Revolution some Massachusetts and Rhode Island pewterers adopted their State seals for trade-marks, but the eagle was the most popular of all, and was widely adopted. There are collectors who specialize in pewter marked with the national emblem.

But a good deal of American pewter was not marked at all and this was also true of some English pewter that found its way to this country. The marks on other pieces have in some instances been worn away, and many marked examples cannot now be identified, because the name, initials, or symbol of the maker is unknown. From time to time, however, the identity of a hitherto unknown craftsman is established by deliberate research or happy accident and his name is added to the roster of American pewterers. It is discoveries of this kind which make pewter collecting so fascinating. Some of the best examples of American pewter are still mystery pieces, and more such are likely to turn up. The last word on pewter will probably not be written for some time.

It is the dream of most collectors to discover an authentic piece of native pewter made in the seventeenth century, but the chances of making such a find are so dim that the quest is usually only incidental to the pursuit of other pieces. The collector may be attracted by certain forms of pewter and specialize in porringers, tankards, or whale-oil lamps. Again, his chief interest may be in pewter made in a particular region or during a certain period. Or perhaps his main concern is the work of a single craftsman. Collecting pewter can take many forms.

Competition finally killed the pewter trade. The accidental discovery of Sheffield plate in the eighteenth century had done the pewterers no good and cheap china and glassware did even more harm. As these last caught the popular fancy, people gradually became contemptuous of pewter. It looked for a while as if the development of the silvery-white metal called in the trade "Britannia ware" would save the situation. Britannia is in reality nothing but a super grade of pewter made of tin, copper, and antimony. When first introduced about 1800 it was cast in molds, but to meet the popular demand for it the cheaper method of spinning and stamping it was adopted, and elaborate designs were used in imitation of the silversmiths. The discovery of electroplating in the nineteenth century marked the end.

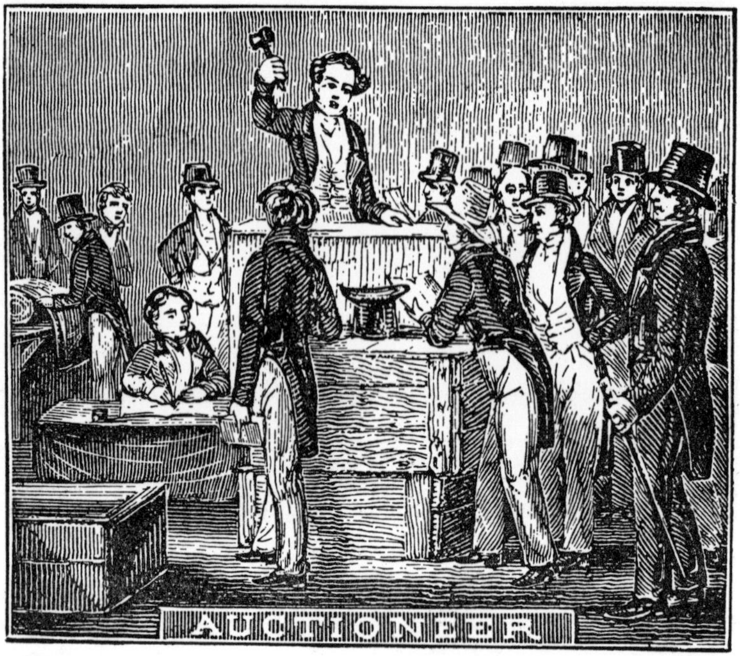

AUCTIONEER

13

Silverware

BEFORE there was any banking system of much account in this country, silverware was regarded as a good investment. From the West Indies and other trade routes Spanish dollars poured into the seaports and river ports of New England, and when a person had acquired a store of this coinage he was apt to take it to the local silversmith to be fashioned into porringers, tankards, teapots, or other articles that were at once useful and beautiful. Everybody tried to build up a silver collection, because if worse came to worst, it could be easily converted into cash. During hard times and wartimes a lot of fine old silver was melted down. It was also done when the owner wished to have more up-to-date pieces of silverware to display on his sideboard.

In working silver dollars into different articles, the silversmith first melted them in a crucible and cast the silver in solid pieces by pouring it into iron molds. Then, after forging the plates on an anvil while not quite red hot, he reduced them still further and to a uniform thickness by passing them several times through steel rollers. Pure silver, which is 1000 parts fine, is too soft for everyday use, but coin silver is only 900 parts fine, and can be worked into durable silverware; though it should be noted that it is not up to the present-day sterling standard, which is 925 parts pure silver, to which copper is commonly added to impart stiffness and wearability. The sterling standard has been fixed for many years by federal law and never varies.

The silversmith had four ways of working his metal —by hammering, stamping, casting, and spinning. The method used depended on the type of article to be made. He had to decide which one was best for the particular job from the standpoint of durability and beauty. In making a piece of hollow ware composed of several parts, he might use different methods for the different pieces. He had to be not only a highly skilled craftsman, but an artist besides.

In making a plain teapot, for example, there were many things to be considered and many steps to be taken. In the first place, the silversmith had to decide what form it should take, choosing a design that would permit the tea to brew properly. The spout had to be shaped so the liquid would pour easily, and care had to be taken not to place it so low down that the tea would rise in it and spill. The teapot also had to be made to allow easy cleaning and have strength and balance.

With all these considerations in mind, the silversmith

formed the body first by cutting the plate in a circular form, placing it on a block of soft wood with a concave face, and beating it with a convex hammer until it had been brought to a form much like that of a saucer. He then placed it on an anvil and beat it a while with a long-necked hammer with a flattish face. He next raised it to the proposed form by forging it on a long slender anvil called a "stick" with a narrow-faced hammer, which spread the metal perpendicularly from the bottom, or laterally, depending on the position in which the hammer was held when it came in contact with the metal. When it had been brought to the desired form it was planished all over by beating the outside with a small hammer while the piece rested on a small steel head inside. During these operations the silver was occasionally annealed by heating it in the charcoal fire, but, except for the first forging, it was wrought while cold.

An ordinary teapot consisted of about fifteen pieces, most of them rolled and forged as described. The knob, the spout, and the handle were either cast or the two parts composing them were cut from the plate and shaped by stamping them with steel dies. The various parts were then soldered together with an alloy composed of about three parts of silver and one of brass and copper. But before the spout and handle were added, the body was polished on a lathe, first with a file, then with a scraper, and afterward with pumice stone. It was next removed from the lathe and held against a rapidly revolving brush charged with fine brick dust and sweet oil. Then, after the handle and spout had been soldered in place, the teapot was annealed and placed in pickle, that is, in a weak solution of oil of vitriol. On removal it was scoured with sand and water and finally burnished with a steel instrument.

All these steps were necessary to make a simple teapot, but in addition the silversmith stood ready to decorate the piece by chasing or engraving. Chasing was done with small tools and punches tapped with a hammer. Flat chasing is impressing the design on flat surfaces, while in *repoussé* chasing the decoration is brought out in high relief by forcing the silver out from the inside and modeling the details from the outside by pressing back parts of the raised surface. Engraving is another form of hand decoration produced by cutting into the surface of the metal with engraving tools. John Singleton Copley's portrait of Paul Revere in the Boston Museum of Fine Arts shows the youthful silversmith—he was thirty when the picture was painted—sitting at his work table holding a teapot, his engraving tools spread out before him.

It is generally agreed that the silversmiths achieved their best results by hammering the metal, though spinning and stamping silver have been known and practiced since the earliest days of the craft. Spinning is a method of shaping pieces of hollow ware by revolving a flat disk of silver over a wooden or metal form and spreading the silver around it until it assumes the desired shape. Pieces fashioned in this way do not permit the craftsman to impress them with his own individuality as does working with a hammer; it is the difference, albeit a subtle one, between the handwrought and the machine-made article. Besides, as a result of frequent annealings, necessary in the case of handwrought silver to keep it workable and prevent cracking, old plate presents a fine white appearance superior to that of modern manufacture. Connoisseurs prefer handwrought silverware.

The silversmiths were versatile men and sometimes carried on other trades, some being clockmakers, bell founders, cabinetmakers, and blacksmiths. Silversmiths were often called "whitesmiths" because they worked in a metal of lighter hue than the blacksmiths did. There was nothing strange in a silversmith being also a blacksmith. It took a lot of strength to hammer out the cold metal in fashioning plate. One cannot help but notice the large, powerful hands of Paul Revere in the Copley portrait just mentioned. Yet occasionally women took it up. Minerva Dexter of Middletown, Connecticut, was a lady silversmith of the eighteenth century. It has been doubted whether she personally worked with hammers, anvils, punches, beak irons, and other tools of the trade, but she may very well have been a brawny creature.

Silver spoons were among the most treasured possessions of the colonial housewife. They were usually the first pieces of silverware she acquired. In the sketch of his life and habits, Boston-born Benjamin Franklin tells a delightful anecdote of his frugal and affectionate wife, who could scarcely have made a prettier apology for indulging in the luxury of purchasing her first piece of silverware.

> We have an English proverb [he writes] that says, *"He that would thrive, must ask his wife."* It was lucky for me that I had one as much disposed to in-

dustry and frugality as myself. She assisted me cheerfully in my business, folding and stitching pamphlets, tending shop, purchasing old linen rags for the papermakers, etc., etc. We kept no idle servants, our table was plain and simple, our furniture of the cheapest. For instance my breakfast was for a long time bread and milk (no tea), and I ate it out of a twopenny earthen porringer, with a pewter spoon. But mark how luxury will enter families, and make progress, in spite of principle: being call'd one morning to breakfast, I found it in a China bowl, with a spoon of silver! They had been bought for me without my knowledge by my wife, and had cost her the enormous sum of three-and-twenty shillings, for which she had no other excuse or apology to make, but that she thought *her* husband deserv'd a silver spoon and China bowl as well as any of his neighbors. This was the first appearance of plate and China in our house, which afterward, in a course of years, as our wealth increas'd, augmented gradually to several hundred pounds in value.

During the British occupation of Boston, provisions became so scarce during the summer of 1775, and the plundering expeditions sent out by General Gage to procure fresh food were so unsuccessful, that he decided to arrange for the removal of a large number of the inhabitants from the town. Accordingly, notice was given that the names of those who wished to leave would be received, and notwithstanding the restriction that no silverware was to be carried away and no more than five pounds in cash by each person, more than two thousand people handed in their names within two days. But many persons of property who would have been glad to leave were afraid to do so, because they knew the soldiers would take everything they left behind. Of those who departed, many women quilted silver spoons into their garments, and coin was smuggled out of town in the same way.

Collectors often speak of the tiny silver bowls with eared handles holding only a spoonful of liquid as "wine tasters," but George Munson Curtis has pointed out that this is a misnomer, because our ancestors were not wine tasters. They *drank* from tankards, beakers, and caudle cups. The miniature silver containers were dram cups, so called because they held a dram or spoonful of medicine, and people used them to dose themselves. Dram cups were appraised in colonial inventories at less than spoons. They were made of pewter as well as silver.

During the latter part of the seventeenth century and the early part of the eighteenth the most popular spoon was the rattail, which took its name from a ridge bearing a fancied resemblance to the tail of a rat that extended from the handle halfway down the back of the bowl. Although it appeared to give strength to the spoon, it actually contributed little and was probably used merely as a decorative device. The early rattail spoons had oval bowls and the ends of the handles were notched or trifid. Later the handle tips became round, the bowls egg-shaped. In one form and another the rat-tailed spoon was popular for a long time.

The drop or double-drop spoon which succeeded it had a conventionalized shell or other design in place of the rattail, and both the handle and the bowl grew more pointed. Another distinctive change occurred in the curve of the handle, which before 1760 bent forward a little at the end. This became a backward bend. Ornamenting the bowl and handle, which began about this time, was not done by hand, as some have supposed, but by dies which were impressed upon the metal with hand screws or drop hammers.

The spoon with the coffin-shaped handle, which was in fashion during the first decade of the last century, was followed by the fiddle shape. This last type often had a shoulder just above the bowl. No matter what the ruling style might be, each had its variations, though the silversmiths in making spoons usually adhered to the established sizes.

Pre-Revolutionary spoons generally came in three standard sizes, namely teaspoons, porringer spoons, and tablespoons. The old teaspoon was smaller than the one we are familiar with today. The porringer spoon was not so large as our dessert spoon, and the tablespoon had a shorter handle than its modern namesake.

Silver forks are rare because the colonial silversmiths did not make many. Truth to tell, our ancestors ate with their knives and fingers in a way we would not dream of doing today. In a book published in 1868, the author, in commenting on American social life and domestic manners, says:

> Silver forks were first brought into general use about twenty-five or thirty years ago. Those previously used were the common three-pronged steel forks, or two-pronged ones, either of them sufficiently inconvenient for carrying loose food to the mouth. Another improvement, about as old, in table furniture, is the in-

Silverware

vention of balanced knife handles, the weight in the handle keeping the blade off the table cloth when laid down; a little thing but very promotive of cleanliness.

Mrs. Anstice Updike Lee of Rhode Island was impressed by silverware she saw in Connecticut when she visited the state in 1791. In the spring of that year, accompanied by her brother, she rode to Hartford on horseback, the roads being too muddy for vehicles, and put up at Bull's Tavern, where she was delighted by the fresh Connecticut River salmon. She was asked to tea at the home of Colonel George Wyllys with President Stiles of Yale College.

> The mansion I admired; and the manners of the Colonel's family combined urbanity with dignity [Mrs. Lee said later]. The room where we sat was spacious, and there was a greater display of silverware than I had ever seen before. There was a large mahogany table in the parlor, and under it stood a finely-wrought silver chafing-dish, and a silver kettle on it; there was also a large silver tea urn. On the table stood a large silver waiter and a large silver teapot, silver sugar-dish, and silver cream pot. This was surrounded by a richly ornamented set of China service; in unison with that were elegant chairs, carpets, and mirrors. It was impressive evidence of an ancient family of wealth.

The eighteenth century was a far more luxurious period than the preceding century and to meet the requirements of the times the later silversmiths made a much wider variety of articles than their predecessors, whose work was limited to a comparatively few objects, such as tankards, flagons, mugs, caudle cups, beakers, and porringers. Among the things made by the later craftsmen were snuffboxes and patch boxes, candlesticks and candle snuffers, shoe buckles and knee buckles, salt cellars and pepper shakers, cruets and trays, sugar tongs and nutmeg graters, saucepans and sauce boats, cream pitchers and basins, hatbands and thimbles, inkstands and sword hilts. Gold objects included buttons, rings, hair combs, toothpicks, and beads. Trinkets for feminine use in gold and silver were standbys of the trade.

The majority of silversmiths, particularly those in the small towns, kept very few ready-made articles other than spoons and gold beads on hand in their shops. Silverware represented hard cash, to say nothing of the work that went into making it, and many silversmiths simply did not have the money to tie up in manufactured stock. Almost everything was made to order. As the silversmiths in the large and prosperous towns, like Newburyport and Boston, Massachusetts; Newport, Rhode Island; and Norwich, Connecticut, got the cream of the trade, the country craftsmen as a rule had to content themselves chiefly with making spoons and jewelry and only occasionally received commissions for making more consequential pieces. It was not that they did not have ability, because after serving a seven years' apprenticeship they had the skill, but because persons of wealth in the small towns were prone to place their orders with the famous silversmiths in the more populous centers. Many a country silversmith had to turn his hand to other things to make a living.

Some of the best work of the early silversmiths went

into the fashioning of drinking vessels of one kind or another—beakers, caudle cups, mugs, cans, tankards, and punch bowls. It was an age of potent drink for powerful men, but the inevitable reaction set in, and as a result of the temperance movement during the first half of the nineteenth century a lot of splendid old plate of the finest workmanship was melted down and made over into spoons and other articles of a nonconvivial character. Just how fine the old drinking vessels were may be seen by surviving examples belonging to many New England Churches. It is true that some silverware was made expressly for religious purposes, but much of that which was used had seen domestic service before being donated to the ecclesiastical societies.

The Congregational Society of Norwichtown, Connecticut, has a two-handled cup made by John Dixwell (1680-1715), one of the early Boston silversmiths, who was a son of the regicide judge, Colonel John Dixwell, who lived in New Haven for many years under the name of James Davids. But this is not the only association that gives interest to the cup. It is inscribed THE GIFT OF SARAH KNIGHT TO THE CHH. OF CHRIST IN NORWICH, 1772. This was Sarah Kemble Knight, Madam Knight, the author of the famous journal of a trip from Boston to New York in 1704. She lived for a number of years in Norwich, but is buried in the ancient hillside cemetery in New London, near which Benedict Arnold stood and watched the town burn during the Revolution. From the gray stone marking the grave of this remarkable woman I copied the following brief inscription:

> Here Lieth the Body
> of Mrs. Sarah Knight
> Who died Sept the 25
> 1727 in the 62d Year
> of Her Age

She was survived by her only child, Elizabeth, who, when she died a few years later, left a large amount of silverware, jewelry, and other property. It is quite possible that some of the following items from the inventory of Elizabeth's effects may have been inherited from her mother.

> A negro woman, Rose; man, Pompey.
> Indian man, named John Nothing.
> Silver plate, amounting to £234.
> A damask table-cloth, 80s.
> Four gold rings; one silver ring; one stoned ring.
> A pair of stoned earrings; a stone drop for neck.
> A red stone for a locket; two pairs gold buttons.
> A diamond ring with five diamonds (prized at £30).

The punch bowl which Paul Revere made for the Sons of Liberty in 1768 is the most valuable piece of colonial silverware in America. When the Boston Museum of Fine Arts acquired it by public subscription for $56,000 it was stated that the Liberty Bowl would have been worth the money had it been merely a battered relic instead of in almost perfect condition.

Another famous New England punch bowl is the one made for Governor Wentworth of New Hampshire by the Boston silversmith, Daniel Henchman (1730–1775), a contemporary of Revere. It belongs to Dartmouth College.

Silverware

Quite apart from their beauty and charm, it is the historical associations attaching to many old silver pieces that add greatly to their value. In many instances the historic interest is heightened by the important part which the early silversmiths played in the public affairs of their day.

The first New England silversmith of whom there is any record was John Mansfield (1601–1674), who arrived in Boston in 1634. No example of his work has been identified, nor is it known whether he trained any apprentices or not, but it is thought likely that he may have taught the art of working in silver to John Hull (1624–1685), who reached Boston the following year. In 1640 another English silversmith, Robert Sanderson (1608–1693), arrived. In 1652 he became the partner of John Hull. That year Hull was appointed mint master of Massachusetts and began coining the famous Pine Tree shillings and sixpences. The arrangement was that Hull should have one shilling out of every twenty for his services, which enabled him at the time of his daughter's marriage to give the girl her weight in shillings. The minting of these coins, the first made in America, was continued by Hull and Sanderson for thirty years.

Jeremiah Dummer (1645–1718), who achieved prominence as a silversmith, learned his trade under Hull, as did Timothy Dwight (1654–1691), another Boston silversmith. Dummer's brother-in-law, John Coney (1655–1722), was either an apprentice of Hull or of Dummer. Anyway, he was outstanding. One of his apprentices was the father of Paul Revere.

There were scores of silversmiths at work in New

England during the eighteenth century. Names well known to collectors are John Burt, John Coburn, Jacob Hurd, John Noyes, John Edwards, and Edward Winslow. All these were Boston silversmiths and most of them had sons to carry on their businesses. Others in other places were William Moulton of Newburyport, Samuel Vernon and Jonathan Otis of Newport, Pygan Adams of New London, and Jacob Sargeant of Hartford.

Perhaps the most remarkable record for longevity in the silver business is that of the Moulton family of Newburyport, who for six generations, covering a span of nearly a century and a quarter, handed on the business from father to son. William Moulton (1664–1732), who founded the business in 1690, was a black- and whitesmith. Finding a demand for his silverware, he taught his son Joseph the craft, who in turn taught his son William, and so on. There were three Williams and three Josephs in direct line of descent who were silversmiths. Nor did the business die when the Moultons were through. Two apprentices of the last Joseph carried it on. One of these was Anthony Towle, and the Towle Silversmiths are still making silverware in Newburyport today, carrying on the traditions of fine craftsmanship which began with the first Moulton two hundred and sixty years ago.

Paul Revere is, of course, the most celebrated American silversmith. This is not because of his nocturnal ride immortalized by Longfellow, but because he was a genuine artist in silver whose work was not only unsurpassed by his contemporaries, but also measured up to that of the best English craftsmen of the time. It is significant that during World War II the Goldsmiths and Silversmiths Company of London paid tribute to Paul Revere and his work. Revere's companion on the midnight ride was also a Boston silversmith, William Dawes, who helped to spread the alarm. Revere, in addition to pitchers, punch bowls, teapots, candlesticks, and flagons, made silver dental plates "of real use in Speaking and Eating." He was a versatile man, and eventually gave up silversmithing to become a coppersmith and bell founder, but his greatest work was in silver.

It is only within the last half century or so that collectors have taken any interest in old American silver. Before that, it was generally assumed that practically all the silver to be found here was English, but most of it was actually American. This seems to have been first pointed out by Dr. Theodore W. Wolsey in an article in *Harper's Magazine* in 1896. Interest was further stimulated by the magnificent exhibition of silverware at the Boston Museum of Fine Arts in 1906, which was a revelation to most of those who saw it.

One reason, perhaps, why people had been misled into thinking that there were scarcely any silversmiths in this country was because the craftsmen of the period followed more or less closely the changing fashions in English design. Yet they were not slavish copyists, but adapted the designs to American taste, which demanded simple lines and good proportions. Fortunately, these silversmiths were fancy free and did not try to follow the elaborate and flamboyant ornamentation that was characteristic of some of the silver made abroad in the eighteenth century. Another factor which may have thrown people off the track was the high quality of the workmanship. Apparently people could not believe that such excellent work could be that of provincial silversmiths.

Old silver is identified by the hallmark of the maker. In England it was the official mark of the Goldsmiths' Company which was stamped on gold and silver articles to indicate that the standard of purity set at the Goldsmiths' Hall had been adhered to by the maker. There were no laws in the colonies establishing a standard, perhaps because the silversmiths were men of integrity and standing in their communities, and it was felt that regulations to prevent fraud were unnecessary. The silversmiths proved worthy of the faith that was placed in them. In marking silver they used their names or initials, often with the device they had adopted as a trade-mark. John Coney of Boston used a rabbit, a cony or coney being a rabbit. The word COIN was also sometimes used. It was not until about 1865 that the word STERLING was first employed as a hallmark. It is now required by law and indicates that the metal is up to the government standard for what is often called "solid silver."

It is not surprising that New England, which in the early days produced more silverware than any other part of the country, should still be the center of the trade. The manufacture of sterling is practically confined to Connecticut, Massachusetts, and Rhode Island. In 1917 the New England silversmiths formed a guild,

The Sterling Silversmiths Guild of America, with the following companies as members:

> The Alvin Corporation, Providence, Rhode Island.
> The Gorham Company, Providence, Rhode Island.
> International Silver Company, Meriden, Connecticut.
> Lunt Silversmiths, Greenfield, Massachusetts.
> Reed and Barton, Taunton, Massachusetts.
> The Towle Silversmiths, Newburyport, Massachusetts.
> R. Wallace & Sons Manufacturing Company, Wallingford, Connecticut.

These companies still make many of the old patterns first used by the colonial silversmiths and now as then New England silverware is a good investment.

GLASS BLOWER.

14

Old New England Glasshouses

WHO invented glass or at what period it was discovered is quite unknown. It is made of sand, lime, and soda, to which other ingredients are added, depending on the kind of glass produced, and the probability is that it originated in Egypt or Asia Minor as long ago as 4000 B.C.

Its history in New England dates from the building of a glasshouse in Salem in 1641. Two years before this Obadiah Holmes and Lawrence Southwick, seeing the need for such an industry, had formed a partnership and the following year enlisted the help of an experienced glassman named Ananias Concklin. They were able to get financial assistance from the town and in due time the first batch of glass was melted and blown into bottles. Production continued erratically for a couple of years and the fires were then drawn. Whether they were ever lighted again or not is a moot question. An attempt was made to reorganize the industry in 1645, and in the opinion of some people glass continued to be made occasionally until 1661. But others believe that the only manufacturing done was between 1641 and 1643. The one thing which seems clear is that the venture was not a success. Few if any of the bottles made at the Salem glasshouse are known to exist.

More than a century later, in 1748, a German named Joseph Crellins promoted a scheme to establish glassworks in the Berkshire towns of Lee and Williamstown. There was a plentiful supply of wood at hand for the furnaces, and the sand of the region was suitable for glassmaking, as we know from its having been used later at the famous Sandwich Glass Works on Cape Cod. But the German glassworkers whom Crellins proposed to employ did not arrive within the time granted by the colonial government for their entry into the province, and the project collapsed.

Undaunted by this failure, Crellins interested a number of prominent Bostonians in establishing a glass industry at Quincy. Elaborate plans were made; an ambitious glasshouse and subsidiary buildings were designed, and a village for the glassworkers was projected. A furnace and a small pot house were actually built, but by that time all the money had been spent and the promoters were glad to lease the property.

More money was poured in by the new proprietors, Joseph Palmer and Richard Cranch, who had even grander ideas than Crellins and his colleagues. For they intended to launch a diversity of industries alongside the glassworks, including a pottery, a salt works, a chocolate mill, a spermacetti plant, etc. They fared no

Old New England Glasshouses

better than the original promoters. They could not sell their bottles after they were blown, and a disastrous fire destroyed much of the property.

Fire also wrecked the first attempt to establish a glassworks in New England after the Revolution. This was at Templeton, New Hampshire, where in 1780 Robert Hewes, a young Bostonian, started a glasshouse, employing Hessian deserters from the British Army for workers. The place had hardly got going when it burned. Hewes rebuilt immediately, but the second furnace constructed of stones which had been hauled by oxen from Massachusetts was affected by a hard frost, and at the first firing came tumbling down. That was the end of the Temple experiment. Few examples of the bottles blown there are known.

This did not put an end to Hewes' glassmaking adventures. In 1787 he organized the Essex Glass Works at Boston, with Charles F. Kupfer, a German glassmaker, and others. The company made crown or window glass of superior quality. Its product, known as "Boston Crown," achieved a nationwide reputation, and was in great demand. The company had been called "The Essex Glass Works" because the furnaces were located in Essex Street, but in 1809 the name was changed to "The Boston Crown Glass Company," and two years later a new and larger glass factory was built in South Boston. The War of 1812 ruined the business. The Great Gale of September 15, 1815, destroyed the works. A later attempt at restoration of the enterprise failed.

Robert Hewes, incidentally, was an interesting character. He was what was called a "natural bone setter," like the famous Sweet family of New England, and not only reduced fractures, but marketed a concoction known as "Hewes' Liniment" in bottles blown in his own glasshouse. He had many other business interests, and was also a fencing master, instructing many Bostonians in the art of swordsmanship. He was the author of a couple of military books, *Rules and Regulations for Sword Exercise for Cavalry* and *Formations and Movements of Cavalry*, published in 1802 and 1804 respectively. He was still an agile and clever fencer up to a short time before his death in 1830 at the age of seventy-nine.

There were other early glass factories in Massachusetts, including one at Adams, Chelmsford, Chester, Lenox, and Ludlow, most of them unsuccessful. One or two produced glass for other purposes besides windows, but the chief concern of collectors in these glasshouses is for the "offhand" pieces blown by the workers for their own use from remnants of batches. It was the custom in all glass factories to permit the workers to do this during their spare time.

Before Hewes organized his Boston house there was glassmaking activity elsewhere in New England. In 1783, the year the final peace treaty was signed between the United States and Great Britain, the State of Connecticut granted to William and Elisha Pitkin and Samuel Bishop a twenty-five year monopoly of the manufacture of glass in the state. Backed by this guarantee of freedom from competition, they proceeded to build and put into operation the Pitkin Glass Works at

Old New England Glasshouses

Manchester, which was then part of East Hartford. This was the first glasshouse in Connecticut.

The monopoly had been granted to the Pitkin brothers at the instigation of their father, Captain Richard Pitkin, who had done the State some service during the Revolution. He had a mill on the Hockanum River, where he made gunpowder for the patriot army. Since the government was too poor to pay in money, the permit to build the glass factory and the monopoly were granted to the sons by way of compensation to the father.

The only natural advantage Manchester had for the glass industry was an abundance of wood for the furnaces. The local sand was unsuited to glassmaking, and the Pitkins had to import it from New Jersey, where they also recruited their gaffers or foremen, their glassblowers, and other skilled workers. The sand was brought up the Connecticut River to Hartford in barges, and taken from there to Manchester in ox carts. As the river was closed to navigation during the coldest months of the year, sand enough to last all winter was shipped in during the autumn.

Hartford was then a port of some consequence. It was the trade center of the Connecticut Valley from its headwaters to its mouth and for a large proportion of the state. It had a thriving trade with the West Indies, to which great numbers of horses and mules were shipped. Return cargoes consisted of molasses, sugar, rum, and salt. Enormous quantities of cider were also shipped to the islands and the Pitkins made the huge glass bottles or carboys in which it was exported. These containers, each with a capacity of several gallons, were used to bring back rum and molasses. For ease in handling, the bottles were made with long necks and the bodies were covered with plaited wicker work equipped with handles. These protective casings were made by the wives and children of the glassworkers.

The cider shipped in this way was not the sweet kind that one buys today in grocery stores or at wayside stands. It had been rectified or racked, meaning that it had been distilled into cider brandy or applejack, which was an extremely popular drink in the West Indies.

The Pitkin glasshouse was almost exclusively a bottle works. Bottles were then made by hand, or rather by mouth. The bottlemaker picked up a lump of semimolten glass on the end of an iron tube and blew hard until he had shaped the kind of bottle he wanted. It must have taken a lot of wind to blow one of the Pitkin carboys. It is said that in the early days of the glass industry in Europe glassblowers used to eat quantities of snails to strengthen their lungs.

In addition to these Gargantuan bottles, the Pitkins made endless numbers of flasks of the swirled and fluted types and many other containers in different sizes and colors. The bottles were generally an olive green or light amber. Although I have never seen one, I have been told by local antique dealers that some were cobalt blue. A Pitkin descendant living in Manchester today has, in addition to one of the large bottles and several regular-sized bottles and flasks, a preserve jar and a witch's ball. This same person also possesses one of the very small souvenir bottles which, according to family tradition, used to be blown and given as souvenirs to sleigh riders who made the glassworks their destination in the old days.

Sleighs were used by the Pitkins to get their wares to market in winter when the Connecticut River was frozen. Normally they were carted to Hartford and loaded on vessels bound for Providence and Salem, whence quantities were shipped to the Orient and other places, near and far.

The Pitkins will always have a place in American glass history, because in design and color many of their bottles and flasks are among the best made in the country. The so-called "Pitkin type" of swirl flask and the "Sunburst" pattern originated in the Manchester glasshouse. These types were later produced at Keene, New Hampshire, but the Keene Swirl flask differs in that the swirl is to the right, whereas that of the Pitkin is to the left. The bodies of these flasks were double-dipped and were thicker than the necks, which were dipped only once. Writers on glassware believe the Pitkins were the first to use this German method of producing flasks.

The Pitkin Glass Works continued to make bottles and flasks for nearly half a century. Competition and the exhaustion of the local fuel supply finally brought its activities to an end about 1830. The ruins of the old glasshouse are still visible—a couple of creeper-clad gray-stone walls with several arched doorways or windows. These are likely to be preserved for some time, as in 1928 the remains of the bottle works with some extra land were turned over by the Pitkin heirs to the local chapter of the Daughters of the American Revolution.

Another distinguished Connecticut glasshouse was established at Coventry following the War of 1812, but it did not begin to make a name for itself until 1820, when it fell into the hands of Thomas Stebbins, who was not only a practical craftsman, but an artist with a true feeling for glass. He is credited with introducing the fashion of adorning whisky flasks with the portraits of famous men. His "Lafayette" and "DeWitt Clinton" patterns are presumed to have been made to commemorate the visit of Lafayette to America in 1825 and the opening of the Erie Canal that same year. Production at the Coventry Glass Works ceased in 1847 for want of wood for the furnaces, but the place will be long remembered for its well-designed flasks of superior "metal."

There were other Connecticut glassmaking establishments besides the Pitkin and Coventry works. There was an early glasshouse at West Willington and later another at New London, but to collectors they are less interesting than the other places because of the inferior quality of their product. Poor materials apparently were used and the workers were forever blowing glass with bubbles in it, or "tears," as they are called in the trade. One thing common to the Connecticut glasshouses, as Rhea Mansfield Knittle pointed out in her book, *Early American Glass*, was that none produced window glass or tableware. All the Nutmeg glassmakers were bottle men.

Keen competition was offered the Pitkin and Coventry works by two houses which were started in Keene, New Hampshire, after the War of 1812. One was situated on Marlboro Street; the other on Prison Street. Both were window-glass and bottle houses. After rather uncertain beginnings they prospered, the former under the management of Justus Perry, the latter under that of Aaron Appleton and John Elliott. The Keene bottles, flasks, and decanters were, like the Connecticut bottles, made in different shades of green and amber with some bluish ones. Justus Perry also made black bottles. The most noted Keene flasks were the "Sunburst" and the Masonic. There are several variants of both in different sizes. Other well-known Keene flasks are a "Success to the Railroad," blown to commemorate the building of the Boston and Lowell Railroad, and the "Cornucopia, Basket of Fruit." All are rare, and Keene glass is eagerly sought by collectors. The two houses discontinued operations in 1850 and 1855 respectively.

Two other New Hampshire glasshouses were located at Stoddard. They were bottle works, one built in 1844, the other in 1850, and both outlived the Keene houses. The output of the Stoddard factories was colored glass, and the adoption of clear glass for liquor bottles was a grievous blow to the industry. Many mineral-water bottles, however, were blown and shipped to Saratoga Springs. There is much interest in the glass made in the town, not only the bottles, but the offhand examples as well.

In 1839 the Chelmsford Glass Works, near Lowell, Massachusetts, founded in 1802, moved to Suncook, New Hampshire, because conditions for glassmaking were believed to be better there than at the original location. The business was continued at Suncook until

1850. The panic of 1847 and the lowering of the tariff on European glass were among the things that shattered this glasshouse. It is supposed that the "Lowell Railroad" bottle was originated at Chelmsford in 1829. It was the forerunner of many other railroad bottles, including the one made at Keene.

All the New England states had glassworks at one time or another, though less glass seems to have been made in Rhode Island and Maine than elsewhere. The United States Census of 1840 lists a dozen glasshouses in the region, distributed as follows: Massachusetts four, Connecticut three, New Hampshire three, and Vermont two. Not a great number, but two of them, the New England Glass Company at Cambridge and the Boston and Sandwich Glass Company on Cape Cod, were among the largest glass manufactories in the country.

The earliest Vermont glassworks were at Salisbury and East Middlebury. They began operations during the War of 1812, when the supply of European glass was cut off, and did well for a short time, but succumbed soon after the war. In the eighteen-thirties the Salisbury works, which were situated on the shore of Lake Dunmore, were reopened and operated for a number of years, but they finally gave up the ghost in 1839.

Meanwhile, in 1827, the Champlain Glass Works was established at Burlington. Like most window-glass factories, it produced bottles as a side line—chiefly of a bluish-green hue. The Champlain glassblowers also produced some of the finest offhand examples made in

Old New England Glasshouses

America. The fuel problem proved too much for this glasshouse, and operations were suspended in 1848.

Wood was considered the best fuel for glassmaking, but it took immense quantities to keep even a small glasshouse going. Unless the quality was good, the shearers or furnace tenders had trouble. When proper fuel could no longer be obtained near at hand, the cost was apt to be so high as to force a glasshouse to shut down. Even after the industry went over to coal, the New England glassmakers could not compete with the Midwestern manufacturers, who used lower-cost oil and natural gas. The New England Glass Company of Cambridge, Massachusetts, after a long career, was on this account moved to Toledo, Ohio, in 1888, and became the Libbey Glass Company.

The New England Glass Company was started in 1817 when Deming Jarves, the most famous of all Yankee glassmakers, and several associates bought the plant and business of the unsuccessful Boston Porcelain and Glass Company at East Cambridge. By a special act of incorporation the new company was authorized to make all kinds of flint and crown glass in Boston and Cambridge. Crown glass is simply a good quality of window glass, while flint glass, which is made with lead, can be used for all purposes. Flint glass derived its name from the fact that when it was first evolved in England bits of ground-up flint were used in its composition.

Industry today is not averse to taking people behind the scenes. It raises no objection to letting the public see the wheels go round. But it was different in the nineteenth century, when practically every factory was kept inviolate from the curious visitor, and manufacturing processes were deep and carefully guarded secrets. The discovery of the use of lead in glassmaking in the seventeenth century gave England an important advantage in the world glass market. Clearer and more brilliant glass was made with lead, and English glassware was even shipped to the pioneer glassmaking countries of Europe. The secret of obtaining red lead or litharge was as closely safeguarded as the atom bomb.

Without this knowledge the American glass industry worked under a serious handicap. But to Jarves, who was gifted in many ways, the situation was a challenge. Accordingly, in 1818, he set up an experimental lead furnace at Cambridge, and to the surprise and delight of his colleagues succeeded in discovering the secret at the very first trial. For years afterward he supplied litharge to the American glass industry, and to painters the kind of lead they required.

Born in Boston in 1790, Deming Jarves was only twenty-eight when he made this important discovery. He continued with the New England Glass Company until 1825, when he quarreled with his associates and went off by himself to form the Boston and Sandwich Glass Company, which was destined to make American glass history.

There were several considerations which influenced him to choose Sandwich on the Massachusetts Bay side of Cape Cod for his glassworks. It was not, as might be supposed, because the Cape is a sandy place. The silica there is not adapted to glassmaking. In the early days of

Old New England Glasshouses

the glass industry, supplies of sand were brought from Demerara; later from New Jersey, and still later from the sand beds of Western Massachusetts. The chief deciding factor in favor of the Cape was the fuel supply. The country behind Sandwich was rich in timber, which the farmers were glad to cut and haul to the glassworks at fifty cents a cord. Jarves obtained wood rights to more than twenty thousand acres of land. This wood was mostly small stuff only a few inches in diameter. It was cut to fit the furnaces and kiln-dried. Later, when the glassworks finally went over to coal, Jarves built a wharf on Buzzards Bay and the fuel was hauled by rail across the neck of the Cape, a distance of nine miles.

There were, of course, no railroads when Jarves built his glasshouse in 1825, and this was another reason for choosing Sandwich, as adequate transportation facilities were a necessity. The factory was built on a tidal creek up which vessels could come to the plant with sand, taking it away later in the form of finished glassware. It was twenty-three years before the railroad reached Sandwich. When, a few years later, it raised its rates the glass company retaliated by building a steamer named the *Acorn*, which could cover the fifty-mile run between Sandwich and Boston in a few hours. Both passengers and freight were carried.

In his *Reminiscences of Glass Making*, published in 1865, Jarves told how the glasshouse and the homes for the workers were built in record time. Ground was broken in April and three months later, on July 4, 1825, they began blowing glass. Operations were started with an eight-pot furnace, each pot having a capacity of 800 pounds. Less than 7000 pounds of glass were melted a week, but it took between sixty and seventy men to handle this amount of glass. This was increased as the business prospered and soon there were four furnaces with ten pots apiece. The weekly melt rose to over 100,000 pounds, and employment was given to more than 500 hands.

A great range of interesting objects was produced at Sandwich. Nothing which could appropriately be made of glass was overlooked. Quantities of tableware and many other things were turned out in assorted designs and colors. Plates, pitchers, punch bowls, tumblers, salts, mustards, jugs, bottles, decanters, candlesticks, lamps, chandeliers, inkwells, miniature hats, toy dishes, and different kinds of ornaments were made at this Cape Cod glasshouse. One branch of the business made special glassware for chemists and apothecaries.

Not long after Jarves had launched his enterprise a Yankee invention revolutionized the whole glass industry and caused its rapid expansion. This was the introduction of pressed glass. Hitherto all glass had been blown, just as it had been for centuries, but by the new process the molten glass was pressed into the mold instead of being blown into it. This was a speedier and cheaper method of manufacture which dealt a severe blow to the glassmakers of Europe. They could not compete with the new mass-produced American glass.

Deming Jarves claimed the credit for this invention, but this was disputed by two workers of the New England Company at Cambridge, and the question is one that is still argued, some people supporting one side, some the other. The truth seems to be that experiments were carried on simultaneously in both places and both met with success at about the same time. The controversy got into the courts when Jarves endeavored to patent a press he had improved. In the ensuing contest the Cambridge technicians won.

Although blown glass is more desirable than pressed glass, because of its superior brilliance and luster, the pressed glass of Sandwich is in special request by collectors because of its excellent quality and admirable design. The person responsible for the form and proportion of the Sandwich output was Hiram Dillaway, who for years was Jarves' head moldmaker. The molds used were brass. Dillaway's use of the dolphin motif was particularly meritorious.

Of the various raised designs used on plates, those showing famous persons and events of American history were extremely popular and still are sought for by collectors. Even the small cup plates measuring only three or four inches in diameter sometimes carried historical designs. Stacks of these plates were made at Sandwich in the days when people customarily poured the contents of their teacups into the saucers to cool, and to save the table linen placed the cups on small plates specially made for the purpose. The vogue for cup plates, which it is believed originated at Sandwich, lasted more than twenty-five years.

To meet the public demand, colored glass was made at Sandwich beginning in the eighteen-thirties. Deming Jarves, being a chemist, carried out his own experiments with singularly happy results. The richly colored Sandwich ruby glass is especially fine. It was also at this time that most of what is called "Sandwich lacy glass" was made. By the stippling of a background of a conventional design a lacy effect was imparted to the glass. Both cut glass and etched glass were likewise manufactured on a considerable scale at Sandwich.

For more than thirty years Deming Jarves continued as the guiding genius of the Boston and Sandwich Glass Company. A man of extraordinary ability, not only as a glass technician, but also as a business executive, he nevertheless had the temperament of an artist and in 1858, at the age of sixty-eight, suddenly resigned and went off on his own to build another glasshouse, just as he had done at Cambridge when a young man. But this time he did not go far. He erected his new works in Sandwich near the old plant, and invited the whole town to a clambake to celebrate the opening. He called his new enterprise "The Cape Cod Glass Company," and offered higher wages than were paid by the older glasshouse.

In 1837 Jarves had organized the Mt. Washington Glass Company at New Bedford for his son George, and the Cape Cod Glass Company he intended for his son John, but John died during the Civil War, and Deming Jarves himself passed away in Boston the night of April 15, 1869. When news of his death reached Sandwich the next day the fires of the Cape Cod Glass Company were allowed to go out and were never relighted.

The New Bedford plant closed the following year,

Old New England Glasshouses

but the Boston and Sandwich Glass Company continued operations until 1888. That year the workers went on strike. Warned by the management that if they did not return to work the business would be liquidated, the strikers, thinking the company was bluffing, persisted in staying away. This was a mistake. The plant was closed down and never opened again. Several attempts were made by some of the old hands to carry on the industry, but these efforts were unsuccessful. That same year W. L. Libbey moved the New England Glass Company from Cambridge to Toledo and glassmaking in New England practically ceased.

POTTER

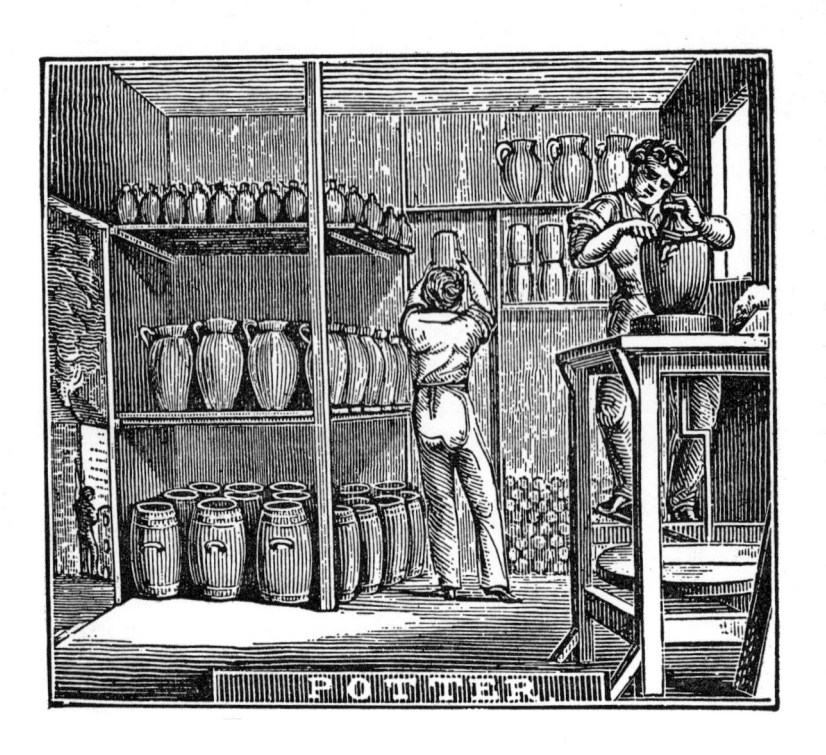

15

New England Pottery

THE first New England potters were the Indians. They knew that baskets could be made waterproof by lining them with clay. Their method of boiling water was to drop hot stones into a clay basket of water. How they learned in the first place that plastic clay when dried became a hard substance is not known, but it has been conjectured that they must have noticed when they left their footprints in soil of a clayey character that the impressions were preserved when the sun dried and hardened the clay. Nor could they have failed to observe that when their weapons, or other implements, came in contact with clay it stuck to them, dried on, and was hard to get off. This or something of the kind is doubtless what happened among primitive peoples in different parts of the world in prehistoric times.

During the colonial period most of the pottery used in New England was imported. This supply was supplemented by a few native potters who worked here and there making the humblest kind of domestic ware for local requirements. Most of it was crudely conceived and poorly executed, but it was handmade, and for this reason has today an ornamental value appreciated by people who care for antiques. A century or so will dignify and add quaintness to almost anything, if you leave it alone.

The New England potteries when they finally got going in the nineteenth century were chiefly concerned with the manufacture of useful pieces, such as crocks, jars, jugs, pots, mugs, pitchers, and the like. It is difficult to realize now how extensively they were used by the housewife in olden times. It required a lot of them just to store the winter supply of food for a large family. Quantities of mincemeat, pickles, and preserves were kept in huge crocks in the cellar. Pantries were crowded with other purposeful vessels—jelly molds and mixing bowls, nests of pots and stoneware bottles. The writer's grandmother kept doughnuts in constant and ample supply in a dark-brown earthenware crock with an earthenware cover and knob in her pantry. Many pottery vessels were used for cooking. The Yankee bean pot was as indispensable an adjunct of the old-fashioned New England household as the family Bible.

The pioneer potters seldom attempted things of a purely ornamental character, such as would now be described as art ware. Yet even their utilitarian pieces were generally given a decorative touch, perhaps a bird or flower, or just a curlycue, which was added freehand

New England Pottery

with a brush before glazing, in a seemingly spontaneous and carelessly rapturous way. These blue decorations on old gray stoneware are familiar to everyone. The color was obtained from oxide of cobalt. The practice was an attempt to make useful utensils more attractive. Crude as some of the early work undoubtedly was, one feels that some of the potters at least were not unaware that functional designs can take a pleasing form.

Many of the early potteries were literally one-horse enterprises. With plenty of fuel for his oven and a supply of the right kind of clay at hand, the potter set up a pug mill to process the clay he had dug and carted to his workshop. This was simply a large tub in the center of which was a revolving upright post or shaft in which a number of knives were set to grind the clay. A long beam, or sweep, extended from the post out beyond the tub, and to this a horse was hitched which walked round and round, turning the blades and reducing the lumps of clay, which had been moistened with water, to a workable consistency. The job of driving the horse usually fell to the lot of some boy, one of the potter's sons, perhaps, or his apprentice.

Neither primary clays, which are found in the place where they were formed by the decomposition of feldspatic rocks, nor secondary clays, which have been washed away by rain or streams from the site where they were originally formed, are free from impurities, and before the potter shaped a piece of clay he worked and reworked it on his bench, removing every foreign particle. Failure to do this was to court disaster, because the presence in the clay of a pebble or a piece of root generally resulted in the article breaking when fired or a hole being left where it burned away.

Another necessary piece of equipment which the potter made himself was his potter's wheel, which is such an old invention that its origin is unknown. It was a rotating shaft or spindle capped by a horizontal plate or disk on which was placed the clay to be shaped by the potter with his fingers and the palms of his hands as it spun around. The head or disk was rotated by means of a horizontal wheel at the base of the shaft. Four spokes extended from the shaft to the rim of the wheel, and the potter sitting at the machine, which was about the height of a low table, pushed the wheel around with his feet. The disk on which the "throwing" or shaping of the clay was done was about a foot in diameter, the "kick wheel" four feet. Later, the wheel was operated by a treadle worked by the potter with his left foot. A still later improvement was the introduction of a large vertical flywheel, at some distance from the spinning disk, which was turned by a crank in the hands of another person, a belt extending around a couple of spindles rotating the plate. This ancient method, by which most pieces of pottery were made until well into the nineteenth century, is still used in small potteries, and in the large, mass-production plants for making special articles.

Apart from his pug mill, his potter's wheel, and his oven, all of which the potter constructed himself, he needed little in the way of equipment except a few homemade tools of wood and wire and some molds for "slip" casting. Slip is clay diluted to the consistency of thick cream. The potter also made the clay boxes called "saggers" in which the pottery was placed before firing to protect it while in the oven from direct contact with the flames.

The sequence of operations in the production of pottery is the same for most kinds of ware. An object which has been shaped but not fired is said to be in the clay state. It is in the biscuit state when it has been fired once but not yet glazed, and in the glazed state when it has been coated with glaze and has undergone a second firing. Color decorations can be applied under the glaze while the article is in the biscuit state, or on the glaze after it has been fired a second time. If the decoration is added after glazing, the article is fired a third time in an enamel or decorating kiln.

Some kinds of pottery are more or less porous in the biscuit state and absorb liquids. Ink placed in an unglazed earthenware inkwell, for example, will soon disappear. Glazing seals the pores and renders a piece practically impermeable. But even nonporous ceramic ware, such as stoneware, china, and porcelain, is glazed, because glazing makes a smoother and more brilliant surface.

The greatest care has to be taken to see that the glaze and the body of the ware expand and contract at the same rate when heated and cooled. If the body has a larger thermal expansion than the glaze it will contract more in cooling and will be smaller than the outer coat of glazing, which will consequently peel off. On the other hand, if the glaze is more expansive than the body it will in cooling try to become smaller than the body and as a result numerous fine fissures or crackles will appear in the glaze. Every effort has to be made to make the body mixture and the glaze mixture agree with each other, so that "crazing," as it is called, will not occur.

In China the potters deliberately produced crackle ware, featuring the network of small cracks in the glaze as a form of decoration. They even went so far as to rub red coloring matter into the fissures to give them emphasis. This Chinese crackle ware was long considered unapproachable, but a New England ceramist, Hugh Robertson, who devoted his life to rediscovering lost secrets of the potter's art, succeeded in imitating it to perfection, even to the blue under-glaze oriental decoration. The beauty and charm of Chinese ceramic colors fascinated Hugh Robertson, and he experimented until he learned how to make the famous Chinese *sang-de-boeuf*, the remarkable surface color with tints and shades which in the light have the shining brightness of of a dome of many-colored glass. Hugh Robertson worked for twenty years at the pottery in Chelsea, Massachusetts, which was started by his brother, Alexander, in 1866. When the plant was forced to close down in 1889, Hugh joined the Dedham Pottery Company.

The old-fashioned New England winters, despite their length and severity, had their advantages as well as disadvantages. It was safer, for example, to haul certain kinds of merchandise to market in sleighs than in carts or wagons over rough roads. This was notably the

New England Pottery

case with the pottery trade. When the fragile ware was packed in pungs filled with hay or straw it suffered little damage in transit.

Goodwin and Webster, who had a pottery on Front Street in Hartford, Connecticut, where they made stoneware from 1810 to 1850, maintained large warehouses in Boston and Salem, which they kept filled in winter by long lines of sleighs loaded with their product. Their ovens were near the water front and at other seasons they made shipments to various places along the coast by sloop. The sleighs which they used when the Connecticut River was closed to navigation brought back loads of fresh fish from Boston for the local market.

Connecticut took the lead among the New England states in the number and output of its potteries. Nothing but stoneware of a practical domestic kind seems to have been made. Although stoneware, as the name indicates, is dense and hard, it is made from a clay possessing a relatively high degree of plasticity. It can be easily worked by hand and is now used by many potters who specialize in art ware, particularly figures and vases. Originally most stoneware was salt-glazed.

This process, which was first used in Germany, was first employed in England toward the close of the seventeenth century, and in the American colonies early in the eighteenth. This rough-surfaced glaze was produced by throwing common salt directly on the fire as the heat of the oven approached its maximum temperature. The salt was fed into the furnace gradually, about a pound being used to a thousand pounds of stoneware. The heat vaporized the salt, which settled in a fine mist on the pottery, giving it a transparent finish preferred to lead glazing. In order to let the salt vapor reach the pottery, the stoneware was not placed in the oven in saggers but in "open setting." This method of glazing during the bisque firing was peculiar to stoneware. Salt-glazed stoneware was very popular during the nineteenth century.

Toward the middle of the last century stoneware, chiefly in the form of jugs, was made for several years at Ashfield, Massachusetts. The ovens were at South Ashfield. Ashfield is a remote hilltop town in Western Massachusetts, which would seem to be one of the last places anyone would think of establishing a pottery. But there were a lot of cider-brandy distilleries up in the hills and jugs were needed. They were made in assorted sizes of anywhere from one to five gallons' capacity, and I have seen an Ashfield water cooler of truly imperial size.

On many of the Ashfield products the name BELDEN appears, usually as a partner of another potter. Partnerships, many of them short-lived, were common in New England. One would be formed, and then for various reasons, perhaps owing to Yankee temperament or the desire of an individual to be his own unrestricted boss, it would be dissolved. Soon after another would be formed, only to go through the same process again.

Potters' marks are not found on early New England pottery and the problem of identification therefore presents difficulties. Prior to the nineteenth century it does not seem to have occurred to the potters to mark their wares. When the practice began many of them used a metallic stamp to impress their names or trade-marks in the clay while it was soft. Others printed their names or painted them on the pottery under the glaze after the body had been partly dried. Collectors, who set much store on these marks, view those added after glazing with suspicion. No mark is conclusive evidence of genuineness, but when other indications of authenticity are present it may have corroborative weight. As in the case of the pewterers, there are published lists of American potters and their marks. Edwin Atlee Barber, a pioneer in the field of ceramic collecting, whose *Pottery and Porcelain in the United States* was published in 1893, was the first to attempt the compilation of such a list.

Eventually New England came to have numerous small potteries, like the Ashfield works, which made wares for local needs, but the industry developed slowly because pottery could be imported so cheaply that its manufacture was discouraged. Little was done in the potting line until after the middle of the eighteenth century, and the great days of the trade were centered in the nineteenth. Perhaps the majority of these potteries were not commercially successful ventures, or were only occasionally and spasmodically successful. The product as a rule was not of outstanding quality. It was fit for the purpose for which it was made, and that was about all.

New Hampshire had a number of plants, one of

which managed to survive many years. This was the Exeter Pottery Works founded by the Dodge family in the eighteenth century and continued by the descendants until 1895. Glazed redware was produced, but by using various oxides in the glaze, the color range was extended to include different shades of brown, yellow, and green.

In 1775, Peter Clark established a pottery at Lyndeboro, New Hampshire, where he made various types of pots, jars, and jugs. The clay used came out red after firing, but this was generally covered with a deep-brown glaze. Redware was the first kind of pottery to be made in New England, but as it was coarse and not very tough it was largely supplanted by stoneware. After Peter Clark's death his sons carried on the business. Examples of this New Hampshire pottery are scarce.

There were other small potteries at New Durham, Moultonboro, and Nashua, New Hampshire. The Hampshire Pottery at Keene was a group of latter-day potters, who began making redware in 1871, but afterward added stoneware and majolica. Some original work was produced here before the factory finally closed in 1926.

Volumes have been written about the ceramic history of Vermont because of the important part the Bennington potteries played in the development of the industry in America. The first pottery in the state was established at Bennington in 1793 by John and William Norton. John was a Connecticut Yankee from the town of Goshen. He served as a captain during the Revolution and soon after peace was declared migrated to Vermont,

New England Pottery

which was then the stamping ground of numerous men who had become unsettled by the war. The Nortons started by making redware, but in 1800 commenced the manufacture of salt-glazed and lead-glazed stoneware under the name of the Norton Stoneware Company. John Norton, who withdrew in 1823, was succeeded by his sons Lumus and John, Jr., and for over a century, or until 1894, members of the Norton family were engaged in the business at Bennington.

John Norton's grandson, Julius, entered into a partnership with Fenton and Hall in 1846, but two years later the firm was dissolved, and a new one formed by Lyman and Fenton, who changed the name the following year to the United States Pottery Company. Another plant was built and the business carried on independently of the Norton Stoneware Company.

Under the management of Christopher Webber Fenton the pottery made at Bennington became famous. Born in Dorset, Vermont, in 1808, Fenton was a nephew of Richard Fenton, who established a pottery at Saint Johnsbury, Vermont, the year Christopher was born. This pottery lasted until 1859. The success of the Bennington factory is generally attributed less to Fenton's abilities as a potter than to his business talents. Credit for the production of fine pieces is given to Decius W. Clark and Daniel Greatbach. Certainly one reason for the success of the ware produced at Bennington was that they were not afraid to experiment with new forms. Just what objects will or will not find favor with the public has always been difficult to predict, but Fenton and his colleagues seem to have been fortunate in this respect. A great variety of articles was produced in Rockingham, Parian, and other wares in a wide range of colors. So diversified was the output that collectors sometimes specialize in Bennington pitchers, figures, or other pieces. John Spargo, who has written many books on many subjects, is the author of several fine ones dealing with the work of these potters. The United States Pottery Company closed its plant in 1858. Christopher Fenton died in 1865.

Although machines today do much of the work that was formerly done by hand in the potteries, the skill and craftsmanship of bygone days that has come down the years has lost none of its importance. From the research laboratory come fresh ways and means of doing things that the old-time potter may have dreamed of but did not know. Antique pottery gives one some idea of the artistic heritage of the world's oldest industry.

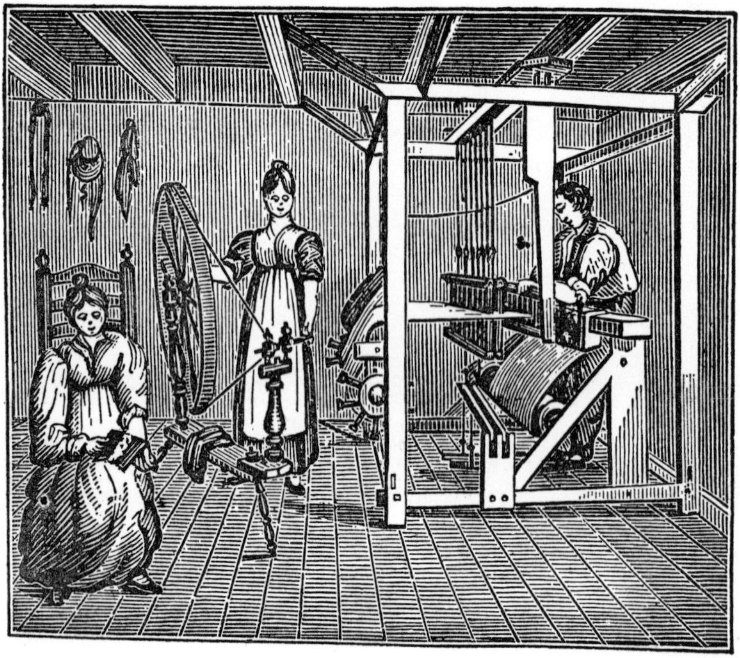

16

The Story behind Them

MANY of the things mentioned in the foregoing pages were part of our ancestors' equipment for living and reflected changes in their way of life and thought. In the development of furniture, for example, one can trace the rise in economic status of various sections of the community. Just as today new living conditions are altering the character of our furniture, so did social changes in the past bring modifications and new developments. Current trends may even be observed in the antiques market.

In our smaller modern homes, with fewer special-purpose rooms, we cannot afford to use space uneconomically. There is no place today for certain furnishings made in the days of more spacious living, and hence we find such things gathering dust in the antique shops. Much as one might like to have one of the large old corner cupboards, with its pilasters, semi-domed top, and carved ornamental shell, which was an architectural feature of many of the homes of our ancestors, there is generally not room for one today. On the other hand, mirrors do not take up floor space. Everybody can use them, and even people with no feeling for antiques are prone to cling to old mirrors that come their way if they are not of overwhelming size. Consequently, it is frequently difficult to find good examples in the shops.

Sometimes new uses are found for old things and articles which have been neglected will suddenly be in demand. Perhaps a person sees in a friend's house an antique cradle used as a receptacle for wood beside the fireplace, and will want one for the same purpose. The idea spreads and a run on wooden cradles results. Or the discovery is made that one of the old leather fire buckets makes an excellent wastebasket, and the price of buckets soars. In the days of volunteer fire fighting every townsman was required to have one of these buckets, and to turn out with it when the alarm sounded. It was usually kept hanging in the hall near the front door, with a bed key in it for taking four-posters apart, and a sack or pillow case for saving small household articles from burning dwellings.

A quaint use to which old iron pots or caldrons used to be put was to paint one red or green, plant nasturtiums in it, and suspend it from a rustic tripod in the front yard. This old New England custom, which predated any general interest in antiques, seems to be dying out, as one sees far fewer now than formerly.

In colonial times people did not own stocks, bonds, and other securities. What wealth they possessed consisted of tangible property, real and personal, and the old wills and inventories of estates usually mentioned everything a person left down to the provisions on hand at the time of the testator's death. The inventories enumerated the contents of houses room by room, and while it is sometimes difficult to tell what some of the things listed in the very earliest ones were, one gets a good idea of what our ancestors had in the way of worldly goods. The following is a portion of the will of a well-to-do settler in the Kennebec River region of Maine just prior to the Revolution. In several ways it is an interesting and revealing document.

> In the name of God amen this tenth day of September Anno Domini 1771 I Samuel Denny of Georgetown within the County of Lincoln in New England Esqr being weak in body but of sounde minde and memory through mercy do make this my larst will and testament in manner following viz in the first and chief plase I give and biqueath my pretious and Emortal soul into the hand of that God who gave it to me praying through the merits and Intersession of the glorious Redeemer I may Receive the sam again at the Resurrection of the Just into Eternal Life and as to my temporal Intrest I give and dispose of the same after the following manner
>
> Itum I give unto my loving wife Catherin Denny fower good milch cows one yoak of oxen yoak and chain ten sheep and the best bed underbed and bedstead together with an Equal share of all that belong to beds both of lining and wooling with the rest of my fether beds that may be in my hous at my deseace both for quantity and quality the looking glass with

black frame tabel and smorl trunck in my Rome in the grate Rome and Elseware the chist of drawers the best tea table and that of my make 6 tea cups and sarsers 1 Tea Kittel shugar dish crempot all these of the best together with the best tongs shovel and belows three puter dishes six best Earthun plat fower best candlestcks the belmettel and brass scilit a pair of Iron dogs 2 flat Irons the boxiron and 2 heters warming pan toster the gret bibel 2 bras chafendishes one large and one smorl spinning wheale 2 puter basins 3 puter prongers 3 brkfas basins 3 wine glarsses 2 bekers 2 bowls all the provision that may be in the hous of meal pork bief flower butter chese talu candels molases shuger cofey tea rise spises chocolet corn and other grain together with all the woole yarn flax lining or wooling not made up sope tabellining all the tin ware all dairey vessels pails tubs and barels hay in barn 1 spade 1 how 1 ax the silver can 6 common puter plats as also what time I may have in Ebenezer Kelly by Indentur together with sute of curtains

The above mentioned artacels and Every of them I give unto my wife for hir to use or dispose of according unto hir own will and pleasure and not be accountable to any furthermore for and towards her comfortable support during hir natural Life I give the and Improvement of my now dwelling hous with all other buildings contiguous together with the land and marsh to the southward of the stone worl nere the meting-hous and the hither dam which Includ Lotts No 4,5,6,7 together with what Land I own on borld head and the marsh to the southward of Newtown bay and crick and night pasture for said cows and oxen in that pasture between the road and the marsh to be improved by hir living on the place and not by a tenant together with a Right to cut firewood on other of my land on Arrowsick Iland & that on the Easterd side of the country road & that for hir own fire only and to be burnt on the premises together with the use and improvement of tobias and Susanah two of my negroes she mainting them in sickness and health together with the crane hooks grate tongs shovel citchen table & clock all the Iron and holow ware & all the chairs together with the smorl bras Kittel and cofey mill with the sum of tenn pounds Lawful money to be paid out of my other Estate yearly and Every year during her natural life & to be paid quarterly if she chuise it that is £2:10:0 per quarter the use of the pew the word ten is so made by me and figurs £2:10:0 the nesary charge of repairing the premises from time to time to be done at the charge of other of my Estate.

* * *

The romance of New England antiques lies largely in the story behind them. When the China trade was inaugurated for New England by the return of the *Grand Turk* to Salem in 1787, with a rich cargo of oriental merchandise, and Yankee ships were going into service to all parts of the world, geography became the favorite study of many New Englanders. Jedediah Morse's *Universal Geography* was a best seller. It was doubtless this new interest, stimulated by the rapid growth of our maritime commerce, which led a Vermont farmer to make the first American spherical charts of the world.

This pioneer Yankee globe maker was James Wilson of Bradford, a small town on the Vermont side of the Connecticut River above Hanover, New Hampshire.

Wilson was born in a log cabin in Francistown, New Hampshire, in 1763, and though he showed a decided bent for knowledge he was constrained by circumstances to devote himself to farming. In 1796 he bought a farm at Bradford which became his permanent home. When he was thirty-six Wilson saw a pair of English globes at Dartmouth College in the neighboring town of Hanover, and resolved to try his hand at making them.

He began with balls turned from blocks of wood which he covered with paper and finished off with all the lines and representations drawn upon them. This crude beginning was followed by a much better method. Covering the solid balls thickly with layers of paper pasted together, he cut the globes into hemispheres, removed the wooden molds, and joined the paper shells together, which he then finished so they were light and smooth.

But how were the spheres to be covered with maps as good as those of foreign make? Procuring copperplates of adequate size for his thirteen-inch globes, Wilson projected his maps on them in sections, tapering them like the degrees of longitude from the equator to the poles and engraving them with such accuracy that when they were cut apart and pasted on the spheres, the edges with their lines and even the different parts of the finest letters matched perfectly. This kind of designing and engraving was much more difficult than plain work, but except for a few lessons from Amos Doolittle of New Haven, the famous Connecticut engraver, Wilson was self-taught. Yet he succeeded in producing globes equal to any imported from abroad.

The story goes that in 1814 he exhibited the first edition of his globes in Boston, where they caused quite a sensation among scientific persons, who perceived that these native productions were well and truly made. "Who is this James Wilson?" they asked. "Where is he?" Wilson, it was said, was reluctant to come forward because of his rustic garb and manners, but the Boston gentlemen knew how to prize his talents and were proud of the honor he had done his country. They encouraged him by the assurance that he would find a ready market for all the globes he could make.

For a short time Wilson continued to make globes in Bradford, but about 1815, in company with three of his sons, who seem to have inherited much of their father's taste and ingenuity, he opened a globe factory in Albany, New York, where terrestrial and celestial globes were made, the latter showing no less than 5000 stars. About 1826 a new edition was brought out, from freshly engraved plates, which marked a great advance over the earlier globes. The globes were made in three sizes—three-inch, nine-inch, and thirteen-inch. The largest size, mounted on a mahogany pedestal with compasses, sold for $46 and $55, the next smaller size for $40, and the smallest for $5. The business was a success, and after Wilson had reached his eighty-third year he constructed an excellent planetarium, engraving the large copperplate showing the signs of the zodiac, their degrees, etc., with his own hands. Wilson, who had three wives and fourteen children, died at Bradford in March 1855, in the ninety-second year of his age. If you happen to come across an old globe in an antique shop, it is worth while looking to see whether it was made by America's pioneer globe manufacturer.

Occasionally one finds hanging in an antique shop a string of magnificent old sleigh bells of the days of Currier and Ives. The story behind the making of these bells is an interesting one. Most of them came from the town of East Hampton, Connecticut, where all kinds of bells are still made, from small tea bells to large marine bells. There is now, of course, scarcely any demand for sleigh bells, but during the last century hundreds of thousands of them were made and shipped from the town in sugar barrels.

The business was started in 1818 by William Barton, who was born in Wintonbury, now Bloomfield, Connecticut, in 1762. His father was a gunsmith and during the Revolution the family lived in Springfield, Massachusetts, but when the war was over they returned to Wintonbury. For several years, beginning in 1790, William Barton worked in New York, making andirons and other brass articles. Then he returned to Connecticut to devote himself to the manufacture of sleigh bells.

Just why he should choose to settle in East Hampton is not clear, but it may have been because on the creek which is the outlet for Lake Pocotopaug there had long been a forge where iron pots, kettles, waffle irons, and coffee mills were made. East Hampton was then the east parish of the town of Chatham on the Connecticut River. The name of Chatham was later changed to Portland, because the quarries which supplied New York and other cities with structural brownstone were situated there. The quarries lay close to the river, which made it easy to load the stone on barges. There were long sheds to house the oxen used in hauling the stone. Spring hiring day, when the quarry owners chose the men to work for them during the coming season, was an important local event. The sleigh-bell factories in East Hampton found it more convenient to ship their barrels of bells from Middle Haddam, around the bend of the river below Portland.

William Barton was not the first person to make sleigh bells, but he was the first to cast them in one piece. It had been the practice to make them in two pieces and then, after adding the core, to solder the halves together. Barton embedded the metal pellet in the sand when he made the mold. Sleigh bells were then made of pure bell metal, the chief ingredients of which are tin and copper. Later they were stamped out of steel or brass. This was a cheaper and speedier way of producing them, but the stamped bells were never so good as the others. They had neither the tone nor the volume of those made from genuine bell metal. The difference is immediately apparent if you jingle a string of cast bells and then one of stamped bells. The sound of the former is richer and mellower and carries much farther than the sound of the latter.

It was a propitious time to go into the sleigh-bell business, as the construction of turnpikes and the improvement of roads was causing a great increase in the volume of highway traffic. People were just beginning to drive for pleasure. It began with sleighs because they were cheaper than carriages, but presently there were light vehicles of all kinds on the roads, displacing many of the slow, heavy sledges and ponderous wagons that had been in universal use. The mania for speed was beginning to take hold. The coming of the railroads stimulated the desire for faster travel.

After William Barton had been making sleigh bells in East Hampton for nearly a decade, he migrated to Cairo, New York. He remained there several years, but eventually returned to East Hampton, where he died in 1849, leaving a number of descendants who continued the business in Connecticut. But the most successful of the half-dozen sleigh-bell factories in the town was founded by one of Barton's apprentices, William Bevin. He began making sleigh bells on his own account about 1830, later taking his three brothers into partnership. Members of the family are still carrying on the bell business in East Hampton, and it was by visiting the old foundry and talking with those who now operate it that I learned about the sleigh-bell industry.

Twenty different sizes of bells were made in a variety of styles and finishes. The common bells measured from seven eighths of an inch in diameter to three and three quarters inches. The so-called single-throated bell had only one slit to let out the sound, a double-throated bell two slits crossing each other. The bells were tied together in bunches of a dozen and sold by the pound as loose bells, or they were riveted or wired to harness straps which were priced according to the number and quality of the bells used. Sometimes all the bells were the same size, sometimes of different sizes. Anywhere from a dozen to five dozen bells might be used, depending on whether they were large or small, and the price ranged all the way from a dollar to eighteen dollars for a set. Some of the bells were plated with silver or gold, others with nickel or brass; but the bulk of them received only a simple polishing, or were given a silver-white finish. William Barton used to polish his bells by rolling them in a barrel.

Then there were chimes, which were open-mouthed, cup-shaped bells set in metal frames ready to be attached to the shafts or the pole of a sleigh. Chimes were also made to be fastened to the hames of the horses' collars or to the saddles. They were like Russian saddle chimes and were called by that name. The best chimes, which often came in elaborate sets, were tuned. They were better suited to smart city turnouts than to the more plebeian species of sleighs.

Many of the New England winter scenes which were used as subjects of Currier and Ives prints were from paintings by George Henry Durrie (1820–1863) of New Haven, Connecticut. Durrie's specialty was snow pictures. Once he made a trip South, thinking the people there would buy his paintings of snowbound New England, possibly on the theory that it was a cooling experience to look at winter scenes in a warm climate. But he was mistaken; the Southerners wanted none of the Connecticut Yankee's work. Yet Durrie's rural landscapes with their bare trees, snow, and chimney smoke rising in the frosty air from the old homestead—with its barns, sheds, and outbuildings shown in detail—were very popular in the Currier and Ives reproductions. The best-known is his "Home for Thanksgiving." This and other Durrie items, sometimes even an occasional original painting, turn up in old-print and antique shops and are quite valuable. He was an able painter, and it is felt that if he had not died at the relatively early age of forty-three, he would have developed into an American artist of great prominence.

On the Connecticut River just above Middletown, Connecticut, and only a few miles from East Hampton of sleigh-bell fame, is a town with the extremely puritanical name of Cromwell. One day two antique dealers from Hartford who were out looking for things to buy came to an old factory near the river in Cromwell. They had no idea what was made there, but looking at the ancient building they became curious, and seeing an old bell on top of the factory, went in and offered to buy it. They were told that it was not for sale, but in talking with the people in the factory they discovered it was the place where many of the cast-iron mechanical toy banks of half a century ago were made. These banks, of course, are in great demand today, some of them selling for more than one hundred dollars apiece. There were none left for sale in the Cromwell factory, but the dealers found there were a good many of the old illustrated catalogues still on hand, showing the different styles of banks which had been made there, and these they bought for next to nothing. It was a good day's work, as they easily and quickly sold the lot for ten dollars apiece.

It would be impossible to cover all the miscellaneous

antiques which may be found in New England. There is a lively trade in them and though they grow scarcer all the time, there are still treasures to be found. One sees the past at its best, and also sometimes at its worst, in the antique shops, but always they are places of warmth and feeling and even entertainment, where history and romance linger pleasantly.